THE LIBRARY W9-ATE-758
ST. MARY'S COLLEGE OF MARYLAND
ST. MARY'S CITY, MARYLAND 20686

THE EAST EUROPEAN PREDICAMENT

The Royal Institute of International Affairs is an unofficial body which promotes the scientific study of international questions and does not express opinions of its own. The opinions expressed in this publication are the responsibility of the author.

The Institute and its Research Committee are grateful for the comments and suggestions made by Michael Kaser and George Schöpflin, who were asked to review the manuscript of this book.

Peter Summerscale is a member of the British diplomatic service. This volume is based on research conducted during a year's secondment to the Royal Institute of International Affairs. The author uses only published sources and the opinions he expresses are entirely personal and should not be taken as reflecting official views.

THE EAST EUROPEAN PREDICAMENT

Changing Patterns in Poland,
Czechoslovakia and Romania

Peter Summerscale

Published for
The Royal Institute of International Affairs
by
St Martin's Press   **New York**

© Peter Summerscale 1982

All rights reserved. For information, write:
St. Martin's Press, Inc., 175 Fifth Avenue, New York, NY 10010
Printed in Great Britain
First published in the United States of America in 1982

ISBN 0 312 22474 5

Library of Congress Cataloging in Publication Data

Summerscale, Peter.
  Changing patterns in Eastern Europe.

   1. Europe, Eastern - Politics and government.
   2. Europe, Eastern - Foreign relations.
   I. Title.
DJK50.S95   320.947   81-9400
ISBN 0 312 22474 5   AACR2

Contents

Preface

My aim in writing a book on Eastern Europe has been to help explain recent changes by bringing together political, economic and social factors. I have been both lucky and unlucky. The luck has been that the dramatic developments in Poland, which took place after my research at Chatham House began, have given the book a focus it would otherwise have lacked. The less happy aspect is that events have moved extremely rapidly, and daily changes in the political and economic scene have greatly complicated the task of assessment. Most of the draft was completed in the first half of 1981, though a few subsequent updatings (mainly on economic points) have been included.

In undertaking this book, I have been aware of my relative lack of East European background. I hope that this may be compensated by freshness of approach and breadth of perspective; the international dimension is familiar to me mainly as a result of my CSCE experience.

I am grateful to the Foreign and Commonwealth Office for allowing me a generous year's sabbatical, and to Chatham House for the help offered and the excellence of the facilities provided. Amongst those in the academic world who aided me, my particular thanks go to Professor Hugh Seton-Watson of the School for Slavonic and East European Studies, University of London, and to Mr George Schöpflin of the London School of Economics.

I am additionally grateful to the Foreign and Commonwealth Office for giving permission to publish a book of this nature. In this context, I would emphasize that while it is true that the study includes criticism of East European practices, this criticism is intended to be not negative but constructive. Notwithstanding the setbacks which détente has recently suffered, I continue to hope that the CSCE process may, at least in the medium to long term, help to create a more stable European environment, in which Eastern Europe will derive real benefit.

November 1981   Peter Summerscale

1 Introduction

in Berlin Wall?

Writing in 1961,[1] Zbigniew Brzezinski declared that the Soviet bloc was no longer 'monolithic'. What at that time seemed novel is today regarded as a truism: in the succeeding two decades increasing signs of diversity have been seen in Eastern Europe. There have also been changes in the relationship between the Soviet Union and its East European allies. The ties which the latter states have developed with Western countries, especially during the 1970s, are today a factor of some importance in the context of internal stability as well as in the economic field. The purpose of the present study is to assess the degree and significance of the changes in alignment which have taken place, particularly in the last two decades. It also attempts to look ahead. The study focuses principally on external relations, including their economic and military dimensions; it also considers the impact of external influences on internal developments – as the Polish events of 1980 showed, internal and external factors are very closely linked.

Such is the extent of Soviet influence in Eastern Europe that East European studies are sometimes treated in the West as an offshoot of Soviet studies. The present study recognizes the centrality of the Soviet Union in the post-war development of Eastern Europe, but the aim is to view problems primarily from an East European angle. The broad development of Soviet policy is however treated in a separate chapter.

In order to make the task more manageable, three countries have been selected for special treatment: Poland, Czechoslovakia and Romania. These have been chosen because each has a distinctive style and may be said to characterize different tendencies within the socialist alliance.

The choice was not entirely easy: the German Democratic Republic is of course of great intrinsic interest, but its special relationship with the Federal Republic, the complexities of continuing Four-Power responsibilities in Berlin, and the many other ramifications of the 'German problem', render it something of a very special case. The Hungarian economic reform is unique and important, and there are many observers who see Kádár's Hungary as the most viable of the East European states. Although Hungary is not amongst the selected countries, the implications of the 'New Economic Mechanism' are not ignored.

An underlying assumption of the study is that the historical and cultural traditions of the East European states remain crucially important in their implications both as to the suitability for them of the Soviet model of socialism, and as to the pattern of these states' external links. Poland was selected because of its size and influence within the bloc, and also because of its strongly Western-oriented historical, religious and cultural heritage which goes back many centuries. Czechoslovakia was also chosen because of its strongly Western cultural heritage, and because it is a highly industrialized state which in 1945 inherited a large and organized industrial workforce. Romania was included as a representative of the Balkan communist states; it has also been subject to Western influence in the past but its Western heritage is less deep-rooted than that of the other two; its selection also reflects the interest attaching to its 'developing' status, and to its pursuit in the last two decades of an 'autonomous' foreign policy.

Western academics have pointed to evidence of what is seen as a fair degree of congruence between the Soviet Union's inherited 'political culture' and the basic features of its political system.[2] In the case of the more developed East European states, evidence has long been apparent of some disparity between the imposed post-war political systems and the inherited political cultures.[3] While no attempt has been made to make a detailed analysis of this disparity, it is hoped that the treatment of Poland and Czechoslovakia in particular will shed light on this important question.

2

2 The evolution of the regimes

All of the East European states which now belong to the Warsaw Pact have been indebted to the Soviet Union for the fact of the emergence of 'socialist' regimes in the wake of World War II. The significance of the occupation of their territories by the Soviet Army in 1944/5 can hardly be over-emphasized. Yugoslavia and Albania, which were not liberated by the Soviet Army, have both for a time been part of the Soviet bloc, but are not so today; the relative independence of these states owes much to the fact that they were largely self-liberated, as well as to their geographical location on the periphery of Eastern Central Europe.

The pre-1944 legacy

Of the three countries here selected for special treatment, only Czecho-slovakia had a genuinely pluralist political system in the inter-war period: the free society of the inter-war years was one of the few successes of the new order established at Versailles. In Poland, the Pilsudski regime was strongly authoritarian in methods and in general orientation. The Romanian monarchy permitted an ostensibly pluralist political system with the trappings of parliamentary democracy, but the clear trend in the inter-war period was towards authoritarian govern-ment of a distinctly right-wing mould, as reflected in the increasing strength of the fascist-inclined 'Iron Guard' and culminating in King Carol II's reluctant acquiescence in 'monarcho-fascism'. All three countries were strongly affected by nationalism; their educational systems encouraged a crude form of national pride fostering superior and largely hostile attitudes towards neighbouring East European states.

In none of these countries did native communist parties play a major political role in the pre-war years. Communists were the strongest in Czechoslovakia where the party was relatively well organized and built up support amongst the intelligentsia as well as workers; it regularly polled about 10 per cent of the vote in parliamentary elections. It preserved much of its organization during the war years, and the Slovak communists played a large part in organizing the Slovak uprising against the Nazi occupation in 1944. The relative strength of the Czech communists is not hard to explain: alone amongst the East European states, Czechoslovakia has a highly developed industry and a large industrial workforce. In Balkan and predominantly agrarian Romania, on the other hand, the appeal of communism was extremely limited; the Romanian Communist Party, which was declared illegal in 1924, never achieved a mass following. In Poland, with its rather higher – though also limited – industrial development, the Communist Party obtained a few successes in municipal elections but was a less substantial force than the Social Democrats; its membership in the 1930s was about 50,000. In both Poland and Romania, the ruling groups of the bureaucracy were threatened to a greater extent by peasant parties than they were by the Marxist Left.

The assumption of power

The history of the communist takeovers in Eastern Europe in 1944-8 has been well described in a variety of works, and the detail need not be rehearsed.[1] As Hugh Seton-Watson has observed, the Soviet Union had at this time a clear design for the institution of communist control which included the imposition of a uniform Soviet model of socialism through the medium of individuals in whom Stalin and the Soviet Politburo had full confidence. Probably the most important ingredient of success, apart from the physical presence of the Soviet Union, was the establishment of a communist-controlled security police force, modelled closely on the Soviet. It was, perhaps not surprisingly, in Czechoslovakia that the transition to communist party rule was effected with the greatest semblance of legitimacy: in the 1946 elections, which were held in relative freedom, the communists obtained 38 per cent of the vote; the ousting of Beneš in February 1948, by the application of highly undemocratic pressure, could be seen as an unnecessarily summary method of achieving what might have been accomplished more naturally. In Poland, on the other hand, the election organized in 1947 was a travesty of the democratic process: communist victory was won through police intimidation and a variety of forms of pressure and manipulation. In Romania, communists obtained only about one-sixth of the seats in the 1946 elections, but were able to manipulate the National Democratic Front, of which they were a part, so as to secure eventual control. In all three cases, the manner and timing of the communist takeovers were determined to a greater extent by the dictates of overall Soviet policy than by any local concerns.

The subsequent evolution of the communist regimes suggests that, while the circumstances of their creation are not without some importance, the most important factor in their early evolution lay in the nature and degree of the new leaders' indoctrination by and allegiance to the Soviet Union. The communist leaders who came to the fore in Poland had mostly spent the war years in the Soviet Union (Wladislaw Gomulka, who had stayed in Poland during the war, was a notable exception, as was Edward Gierek, who had lived in Belgium and France) and had been well indoctrinated in the Stalinist version of socialism. Rather over half of the Czech and Slovak leaders had similarly spent the war in the USSR. In Romania the situation was different. Of the three most important communist leaders who emerged at the end of the war, two were Moscow-trained (General Bodnaras and Ana Pauker), while the third, Gheorghe Gheorghiu-Dej, was distinctly home-spun. In Czechoslovakia the Muscovites were in the ascendant from the start. In Poland, Gomulka emerged as Secretary-General of the Workers' Party but was forced to resign in 1948: thereafter, until his return to power in 1956, Moscow-trained Poles were in clear control. In Romania, the Moscow and native factions were fairly evenly balanced until 1952, when Gheorghiu-Dej managed to outmanoeuvre his rivals, led by Ana Pauker and Vasile Luca, and purged the Romanian party of their supporters. At the time, Stalin appears to have viewed this convulsion with equanimity, and it is suggested that he may have welcomed the anti-Semitic overtones of Pauker's demise.[2] It was not until later that Gheorghiu-Dej was to emerge in the role of defender of Romanian national interests against the Soviet overlord.

De-Stalinization

In the early post-war years all three communist regimes — as indeed the other East European regimes with the exception of post-1948 Yugoslavia — were carbon copies of the Soviet Stalinist system, complete with police terror, massive purges and the cult of personality. Inevitably, when changes began to occur in the Soviet Union following Stalin's death, their impact was keenly sensed in Eastern Europe. The ambiguities of the 'New Course' introduced by Malenkov caused confusion in Eastern Europe. They also produced great uncertainty, which was to lead to the events in Poland and Hungary of 1956. When Khrushchev assumed the leadership in 1955, it became clear to all of the East European leaders that de-Stalinization in Khrushchev's perception encompassed both the nature of Soviet relations with Eastern Europe and the common model of socialism as elaborated in the Soviet Union. Particular attention was paid to the Soviet recognition of 'separate paths to socialism' in Khrushchev's speech to the Twentieth Party Congress and in the 1955 Belgrade Declaration marking the first reconciliation with Yugoslavia. But the Soviet concept of 'separate paths' was shrouded in considerable ambiguity. The East European leaders were given to understand clearly enough that they were *not* being given licence to imitate the Yugoslav political and economic model — but little positive guidance was offered about the limits of acceptable 'separate' development. And it was hardly surprising that when party leaders were confused, the populations at large should experience a still greater sense of bewilderment.

'National communism' emerged victorious in Poland in 1956 in the wake of internal turmoil which had shaken the communist leadership and after Soviet military intervention had only narrowly been avoided.[3] Gomulka's return to power was followed by the adoption of internal policies which diverged in some significant respects from the Soviet (most notably in the de-collectivization of agriculture and in establishing a *modus vivendi* with the Church). The forces which produced this outcome were broadly similar to the forces in Hungary which led to Soviet intervention and bloodshed; they included traditional nationalism, anti-Soviet sentiment, the yearning for intellectual and cultural freedom, and a desire to create a less repressive political system and a more efficient economy. The challenge to the regime came from virtually all groups in society: workers, intellectuals, students. The explanation for the difference in the Polish and Hungarian experience lies in a variety of factors. Probably, however, the most important was that whereas the Hungarian Communist Party disintegrated under pressure, and invited Soviet intervention as the only means of survival, the Polish party managed to hold together and to work out its own solution. Poland was also fortunate in having Gomulka, so to speak, waiting in the wings, ready to emerge as a *deus ex machina*. The fact that the Soviet Union adopted a relatively low profile in Poland, with Khrushchev agreeing to underwrite the choice of Gomulka during his crisis visit to Warsaw in October 1956, was a tribute to the Polish party's ability to confront the Soviet leadership with a clear alternative of its own. In Hungary, Khrushchev found himself compelled to make his own choice of successor to Nagy. While no Western observers came near to predicting this at the time, Kádár was to prove close to Gomulka in his conception of internal national development — though in the realm of intra-bloc relations and foreign affairs his approach was rather less imaginative and more circumscribed.

While 1956 was a watershed in Hungary and Poland, it was not a year of major change in Czechoslovakia, or in Romania. In both of these very disparate countries, de-Stalinization was to take distinctly less dramatic forms. Czechoslovakia witnessed the curious phenomenon of having show trials of the classic Stalinist variety continue into the year after Stalin's death. The Czechoslovak Communist Party, led by Antonin Novotný, a colourless though organizationally able *apparatchik* whose chief claim to popularity lay in his internment in concentration camps during the war, moved slowly and unenthusiastically in the direction of de-Stalinization. Gottwald was denounced as a protagonist of the cult of personality; after the Twentieth Party Congress it was admitted that some — though by no means all — of the charges against Slansky and other victims of the 1950-54 trials had been misconceived. It was not however until 1963 that the Czechoslovak Communist Party instituted thoroughgoing investigations into the trials which resulted in the rehabilitation of most of their victims. Meanwhile, the Novotný regime proceeded with policies in the internal political and economic realms (including the rapid development of heavy industry and forced collectivization) which were in essence little different from those of Gottwald; appropriately, the huge statue of Stalin in central Prague was left standing.

The reason for the very different pattern of development in Czechoslovakia and Poland doubtless lies to some extent in differences of national character: the romantic, volatile and nonconformist temperament of the Poles was more quickly and profoundly affected by changes in the Soviet Union. Another factor was the rather greater relative strength of the Czechoslovak Communist Party and of its hold over the country. Whereas during Stalin's lifetime the Polish Workers' Party had been as Stalinist and uncompromising in its methods as any bloc party, there were from the beginning significant elements within it which were realistically conscious of the fact that the party lacked deep roots and that frontal assault was not necessarily the best tactic for neutralizing the many non-communist forces remaining in Polish society — which included the still powerful Catholic Church and the majority of the peasant farmers. Another element was that, whereas in Czechoslovakia workers were generally responsive to discipline and authority, Polish workers were distinctly more disposed to take action to further their interests (for a discussion of the reasons for this difference, see Chapter 6). The riots in Poznan in June 1956 were one of the major catalysts of change in Poland.[4] Although in Czechoslovakia some demonstrations were staged against the regime in 1956, mainly by students, these were relatively low key, and there were no major actions by workers.

Meanwhile in Romania Gheorghiu-Dej steadily consolidated his power within the Romanian Workers' Party. During Stalin's lifetime he posed as a staunch Stalinist and a devoted friend of the Soviet Union. In the early 1960s he laid increasing stress on Romanian national interests and his relations with the Soviet leaders became less than smooth. In 1958, he embarked on an ambitious economic policy the aim of which was to develop Romania into an industrialized state, able to hold its own with its more developed East European associates. The stress he placed on the development of heavy industry, and his assumption that the Soviet Union should be prepared to bear part of the burden of this immense task, did not coincide with the vision of the Khrushchev leadership, which was developing its own theory of the 'socialist international division of labour'; according to this, the development of heavy industry was to be the preserve of the already industrialized East European states, while Romania and Bulgaria would constitute the 'market garden' element. Although this issue was not to cause serious friction with the Soviet Union until the early 1960s, Romania's autarkic development stance can be dated from as early as 1956.

During the 1950s, Romania experienced none of the internal turmoil suffered by Hungary and Poland. De-Stalinization in Romania was superficial in the extreme; Gheorghiu-Dej's internal policies were little influenced by the changes in the Soviet Union, and there was no relaxation either in the tight control he exercised over the Romanian Workers' Party or in Romania's Stalinist police controls. The contrast between developments in Romania and those in Poland can be partly explained in terms of the very different historical and cultural backgrounds of the two countries: in Romania the relatively small intelligentsia had no firm tradition of independent thought and action in relation to authority, and was more easily amenable to totalitarian controls (which, from the 1960s, the Bucharest leadership sweetened with a nationalist coating); the inter-war years had produced a privileged cultural elite but not a politically mature society. It can also be argued that authoritarian methods were unavoidable in order to accomplish the rapid modernization of the country: the crash programme of industrialization on which Romania embarked in 1958 called for many years of austerity and sacrifices on the part of the population at large.[5] (While in Poland the intelligentsia was politically inexperienced, it was much larger in size and was more independent and sophisticated in general approach.)

Gheorghiu-Dej was not, however, entirely oblivious to the significance of Khrushchev's speech to the Twentieth Party Congress: he was quick to perceive the way in which Khrushchev's recognition of 'separate paths' to socialism could be exploited to his and to Romanian advantage, by increasing the scope for autonomous action in external relations. The first moves in this direction were however cautious; although Romania was successful in securing in 1958 the withdrawal of Soviet troops from Romanian territory, this was not viewed at the time as betokening any major shift in Romanian-Soviet relations. It may in fact have been considerably assisted by the support given by Romania to the Soviet intervention in Hungary in 1956. It was not (as is described in Chapter 4) until the Sino-Soviet dispute erupted in the early 1960s that the Romanian government adopted a high profile in the pursuit of independent foreign policy objectives.

Differing patterns of evolution

It is arguable that during the new era in inter-communist relations inaugurated by Khrushchev's Twentieth Party Congress speech the leaders of both the Romanian and Polish communist parties were aiming to extract the maximum national advantage; but that whereas the Poles opted in 1956 for an internal model which departed in some quite significant respects from the Soviet, the Romanians maintained an old and obsolescent Soviet model while (from the early 1960s) asserting their national aspirations through an assertive external posture.

There has in fact been a certain consistency in the way in which the two countries have continued, since 1956, to follow these very disparate paths of national self-expression. Although the extremely high expectations raised in 1956 of a genuinely Polish way to socialism were in many respects disappointed, the two major achievements of Gomulka's early years – decollectivization and a *modus vivendi* with the Church – have continued to provide the foundation for a coexistence between communism and other forces in society which is unique in the communist world. In Romania, the expectations engendered by Gheorghiu-Dej in the 1950s were relatively modest, except in the sphere of national economic development. The aspirations embodied in an ambitious Romanian foreign policy found increasing expression during the 1960s and 1970s, although the Romanian leaders were always conscious of the fact that Soviet tolerance might have its limits, and were ready to beat tactical retreats.

Czechoslovakia has been the bloc country with the least consistent internal pattern in the last two decades. From 1962, when pressures on the ageing and increasingly isolated Novotný began to gather momentum, until the Soviet military intervention in August 1968 and Dubček's subsequent demise, Czechoslovakia was a seedbed of liberalizing and humanizing influences. The Czechoslovaks embarked on radical decentralizing economic reforms of a kind which could have become the model for all of the more developed members of the camp. The six-month experiment of reform communism complemented economic reform with an attempt to democratize political life, and to make the selection of communist party functionaries genuinely democratic. Although the reformers wished the communist party to retain a leading influence in the conduct of affairs, they were prepared to extend the political system to include real participation by non-communist elements. They were also prepared to tolerate an uncensored press. In the foreign field, the reformers showed eagerness to develop economic and political relations with Western nations. Some, most notably Ota Sik, believed that the development of trade with the West was the key to Czechoslovakia's emergence from economic stagnation.

The main inspiration for the Czechoslovak reforms came from men in their forties who had grown up with the communist system and whose only other experience had been of the Nazi occupation they were also aware of their fathers' part in having so passively acquiesced in the cession of national territory in 1938. While not anti-Soviet, they had experienced the evils of Stalinism and the feeble attempts of Novotn to de-Stalinize while maintaining intact most of the features of the institutional and political system established by Gottwald. Part of the explanation for the impetuousness of the reform movement lay in the fact that, despite relative tolerance of reformist views on the part of the Novotný government, in its later years, the liberating influences unleashed by Khrushchev's Twentieth Party Congress speech had for so long been denied any outlet for practical application. The further changes in Soviet outlook evident from the Twenty-second Party Congress reinforced those trends. The reformist intellectuals were also influenced by the clear evidence that emerged of failure in the economic system to allow a successful transition from extensive to intensive growth: the fact that the national income actually dropped in 1963 came as a severe shock to economists and others. The Czechoslovak party as a whole was shaken by the manifest signs of economic failure and reform ideas germinated within it, as from the Twelfth Party Congress in 1962.

As it turned out, the 1968 reforms had barely been launched when, in the wake of the Soviet military intervention, the whole process of liberalization was to be reversed under the leadership of the Soviet-installed Gustav Husák. The only lasting achievement of the Prague spring has been the introduction of a federalized administration, the effect of which has been to benefit Slovakia in terms both of economic advantage and of Slovak participation in national life. The proposals for democratizing reforms contained in the April 1968 'Action Programme' of the Czechoslovak Communist Party were totally abandoned, and the ambitious economic reform was put into reverse from 1969. Stringent censorship was reimposed, and manifestations of dissent were harshly punished. The Czechoslovak Communist Party was subjected to a thoroughgoing purge in which reformist elements were ruthlessly weeded out: no less than half a million party members were expelled in 1969–79.[6]

The totality of the Czechoslovak about-turn since 1968 clearly owed much to the circumstances of the Soviet military intervention, and to its repercussions on the Czechoslovak Communist Party. In 1968, reformers were in the clear ascendant in the Czechoslovak party: according to one authoritative estimate, 80 per cent of the delegates elected in June and July to the party congress were 'reform communists' (the remaining 20 per cent being split equally into 'conservatives' of the Bilak/Indra variety, and into 'radical reform' communists).[7] The reformers in the party, no doubt encouraged by their numerical strength as well as by their popularity in the country as a whole,[8] held together well during the events of the summer of 1968 and refused to concede that the blueprint for reform in the 'Action Programme' had been misconceived in its essentials. It was in effect the intrinsic weakness of the conservative elements in the party, and the fact that in 1968-9 their ascendancy was so patently linked with Soviet desiderata, that rendered so difficult any internal policy based on compromise and national reconciliation. The differences between the Hungarian post-1956 and the Czechoslovak post-1968 experiences, at first sight paradoxical, are also instructive. In Hungary, Kádár was able to evolve a surprisingly effective national compromise after the Hungarian Communist Party had virtually disintegrated. His success derived partly from the backing given him by the Soviet Union, which was prepared to allow him relatively free rein in shaping the HSWP in an anti-dogmatist mould. (The process was in fact a gradual one, with the dogmatists in the party only purged in 1962.) In Czechoslovakia, on the other hand, the notable cohesion of the Czechoslovak party, and the close identification of the majority of its leaders with a national reformist line of development, made a Kádár-type solution virtually impossible, once the Soviet leadership had set its face against the Dubček line. After 1969, the division of the Czechoslovak party into Husák and Bilak-Indra wings also tended to limit the scope for movement.

The Romanian Communist Party has not undergone any major changes of direction since Nicolae Ceauşescu replaced Gheorghiu-Dej as its First Secretary. Ceauşescu has further refined the nationalist, Romania-first policies of his predecessor, whose protégé he was. The total loyalty of the Politburo[9] was quickly assured, and the national Romania-first ambitions of the new leader were illustrated without delay with the announcement in 1965 of a draft new constitution in which Romania was proclaimed a 'socialist republic'; significantly, the foreign policy section of this contained no specific reference to the Soviet Union.[10] Heavy emphasis continued to be placed on the country's industrialization. In 1971, the distinction between party and government posts was virtually eliminated, with Ceauşescu combining the posts of President and Secretary General. The only serious sign of political of social unrest encountered during the 1970s was the eruption of workers' discontent in the Jiu Valley strikes of 1977. The regime ascribed some of the blame for this to the loss of contact by party and state officials with workers' opinion at local level, a consideration which was partly responsible for its recent attempt to reform the system of economic management. Political dissent has been little evident although, as is discussed in Chapter 7, this has owed much to the maintenance of a high degree of repression and of strict censorship.

The Gomulka regime suffered a shock in 1970 when workers on the Baltic seaboard staged demonstrations and riots in protest against the announcement of increases in the price of meat and other basic commodities. The government used force against the workers, employing both police and some army units and, according to official figures, the casualties comprised over fifty dead and several thousand injured. Gomulka was forced to resign when it was clear that his policies had lost support within as well as outside the party. The later years of Gomulka's leadership had been marked by increasingly repressive policies, such as the harsh action taken against protesting students in March 1968, and the persecution of Jews in 1968-70, one effect of which had been increasingly to alienate the intelligentsia. Significantly, however, the change of leadership was sparked not by the intelligentsia but by spontaneous action by industrial workers, whose complaint was more basic: in 1965-70, real wages had barely risen, and workers feared that an actual erosion of living standards was in prospect. The new policy of Gomulka's successor, Edward Gierek, was to secure a rapid rise in earnings and in consumption through an expansionist investment policy, bolstered by heavy borrowings in the West. This strategy, although initially successful in boosting workers' incomes, proved to be over-optimistic, especially in the face of increasingly unfavourable trends in the world economy.[11] In 1976, the regime suffered a further challenge to its authority when workers again rioted in protest against a new round of price rises. The repressive action taken by the government against the workers in Radom which seemed to belie the initial promise of the Gierek new course – led to the establishment of what was to prove to be the most effective dissident opposition grouping to emerge in post-war Poland – the Workers' Defence Committee (KOR). Four years later Poland suffered a new major crisis when escalating strikes which spread to almost every region of Poland undermined the authority of the government and led to Gierek's replacement by Stanislav Kania. The occasion was again an announcement concerning the supply (and, in effect, the price) of meat, but the roots went much deeper: the mistrust of the workers, disillusioned by the failure of the regime to fulfil past promises, was reflected in their insistence on including 'political' demands which the government was forced to recognize, most notably in its acceptance of the right to establish trade unions independent of party control. The challenge to the regime was by far the most serious of any since the war.

Generational and systemic changes

In the early post-war period the distinction between home communists and Muscovites offered a key to the priorities attached by different leaderships to national as opposed to 'internationalist' concerns. In both Poland and Romania the phenomenon of national communism owed much to the wartime background of Gomulka and Gheorghiu-Dej. In the Polish case it was strongly reinforced by domestic pressures, including the considerable impact of Khrushchev's Twentieth Party Congress speech on Polish intellectuals, and by the Polish communists' still rankling memory of the occasion when, in 1938, Stalin had ordered the Polish Communist Party to disband itself.[12]

In the 1970s and 1980s, the most important distinction may be between the 'old' generation of communists whose formative years were in the war, and those whose experience derives wholly or mainly from the period of post-war reconstruction. Rakowski in *Polityka* has ascribed the weakness of the party leadership under Gomulka and its failure in 1970 to a 'puritanical concept of socialism', acquired in the conspiratorial and austere environment in which they had functioned in the 1930s.[13] The concern of such men was more with ideological mobilization and the creation of Lenin's 'new socialist man' than with consumer expectations. The emergence of a 'technocratic' team under Gierek appeared to offer the prospects of a radical shift towards the latter, but the results were disappointing. The recently installed Kania leadership in Poland would appear to be slightly more representative of a younger generation which is, in the main, pragmatically inclined; from mid-1981 it has also included men like Rakowski whose pragmatism is reinforced by keen sensitivity to the party's failures, especially in winning working-class support. While in Romania and Czechoslovakia the leading figures are men in their sixties who represent the war generation, when changes come they may go in a similar direction to those in Poland.

Despite a number of changes in their outward manifestations, the political systems themselves have undergone rather limited change since 1956. Perhaps the major change since the early period has been that, as in the USSR, political terror has been replaced by 'administrative' methods of treating dissent which are less harsh and far less arbitrary, although still vulnerable to criticism. Censorship persisted in all the countries with only minor abatement (Poland being the least illiberal in this respect). The Polish leadership in the 1970s showed a greater readiness to tolerate a measure of organized opposition than did their Czechoslovak or Romanian counterparts, but the Polish system itself underwent little change: as in the other two states, the Polish Communist Party maintained its monopoly of power, the one slight anomaly being that a genuinely non-communist and independent political party – the

Catholic *Znak* – was permitted representation of a few seats in the Polish parliament (though by the mid-1970s *Znak* was largely nominal). What many observers have described as the promotion by Ceauşescu of a new 'personality cult' in Romania has not, in recent times, been mirrored in any other Warsaw Pact state (although there were complaints that Gierek had developed a personal style of government in the sense that he shut his ears to all criticism). The extent to which the Romanian President has been able to concentrate power in the hands of his and his wife's family has certainly been a notable phenomenon. It has not, however, altered the fact of the Romanian Communist Party's total monopoly of power: the statement in the 1965 Constitution that 'the leading power in the whole of society in the Socialist Republic of Romania is the Romanian Communist Party' remains as valid as ever.

The formal change in the status of the three states from people's democracies to socialist republics (Czechoslovakia: 1960; Romania: 1965; Poland: 1976) was of little practical significance. In Czechoslovakia and Poland, the announcement of the achievement of a higher stage of development could be said to have been a potential source of embarrassment since not long afterwards serious strains were to appear within their societies (Czechoslovakia: 1962-8; Poland: 1976 onwards). Potentially much more important than any of these changes were the Polish government's concessions to Solidarity in 1980-81, and its apparent intention in 1981 to accord a degree of influence to the Sejm (see Chapter 7).

The major issues

If the problem of minorities is excepted,[14] the communist regimes have faced three major challenges in recent decades: the national issue, that is the assertion of national values and aspirations in accordance with the 'national-particular' in Marxist jargon; the related problems of achieving economic efficiency and improvement in living standards; and the issue of 'democratization' in the limited sense of the perception of a need to evolve methods of government which are more responsive to the real wishes of different groups in society. The effectiveness of the regimes' responses is the subject of subsequent chapters of this study. Meanwhile, a brief summary of the differing past experiences in the selected countries may be useful.

In both Poland and Romania the 'national' issue loomed large in 1956 and the years immediately following. In Romania, there was a notable continuity in the style of leadership with Gheorghiu-Dej and Ceauşescu successively striving to achieve a synthesis between Soviet-style socialism and Romanian national goals as they perceived them.

14

The pattern of internal development did not in fact diverge very far from that in the Soviet Union, and Stalinist methods of effecting control and mobilizing the population for ambitious economic goals underwent little modification. An 'autonomous' foreign policy emerged in the early 1960s, which has continued up to the present. In Poland from 1956 onwards, emphasis was placed on internal goals, with priority being attached to the need to accommodate the persisting preference of Polish peasants for private agriculture and to coexist with the (morally) still powerful Catholic Church: Gomulka and Gierek attempted to reconcile these special features of the Polish situation with the Polish Communist Party's monopoly of power and the maintenance of a close alliance with the Soviet Union. The Polish communists have moved some way from the cruder forms of 'mobilization' of the populace, and have come to rely increasingly on persuasion, while at the same time attempting to maintain the main pillars of Marxism—Leninism. The persistence of a large private sector in agriculture has been especially hard to justify in ideological terms. The main achievement of Czecho-slovak communists was to agree a federal status for Slovakia which went a considerable way to solving the grievances (especially economic) of the Slovaks. The 1968 reform experiment, as is discussed later, was partly aimed at working out a new 'national' orientation for the country in the internal and (to a very limited extent) the foreign spheres; but after 1968 little trace remained of this.

The economic dimension has gained importance in the post-Stalin phase in all countries, but the effects were most dramatic in Poland. Until the Jiu Valley strikes of the summer of 1977, there was little overt sign in Romania of unrest sparked by dissatisfaction with living standards (notwithstanding the fact that Romanian living standards remained, throughout the period, the lowest in the bloc). No attempt at far-reaching economic reform was made. In Czechoslovakia, radical economic reform was a main ingredient of the Dubček experiment but was more a reflection of Czechoslovak intellectuals' disillusionment with the performance of Soviet-style command-economy methods in an already sophisticated economy than a direct response to popular dis-satisfaction; the workers were not, as they were shortly to become in Poland, the major engine of change. The Polish experience was in fact unique: in four successive crises (1956, 1970, 1976, 1980) workers were a leading element (in the last three crises the decisive element) provoking change. Workers' protest was also an obstacle to economic reform: Gierek's gamble in 1971-5 of seeking growth in living standards through foreign borrowing was made after the 1970 unrest had killed the attempt to introduce economic reform, and was in some senses an alternative to it. The 1970 crisis in Poland gave rise to what was dubbed a 'social compact' between government and workers in which workers' support for the government was contingent on the achievement of steady and perceptible rises in living standards; the crisis of 1980 flowed from a breakdown in the Gierek regime's side of the bargain. In Czechoslovakia, the degree of party control in the 1970s appeared to rely heavily on 'administrative' methods of dealing with expressions of discontent. However, the regime appeared to acknowledge that society's acquiescence in the post-1968 'normalization' was linked with meeting consumer expectations; and it can be argued that in reality the regime came to rely also on a social compact not radically different from the Polish. The deceleration at the end of the decade in the rate of annual increases in real earnings to an apparent drop (in 1979) was therefore the more significant. No far-reaching market-type economic reform was contemplated after the collapse of the 1968 experiment, although a partial administrative-type reform was introduced in early 1981 (the 'Ler Reform').[15]

The issue of 'democratization' appeared the least tractable. In the post-war years the bloc communist parties built up mass memberships (the highest proportion, one adult in five being a party member, was in Romania). However, despite the shift at least in Poland away from Stalinist methods, all the regimes found difficulty in imparting to ordinary party members a sense of real participation in the management of affairs. In Romania, the chosen methods in the 1960s and 1970s were a hierarchical unification of the administrative apparatus, with party and state functions fused, requiring a substantial organizational compression. The (fused) President and Party Leader relied fairly heavily on precept and exhortation in mobilizing the party faithful. At the same time, reliance was placed on a 'science of leadership' designed to avoid the kind of failure in communication between top and bottom, evidenced in Poland in 1970. A main feature of this was the rotation of party officials between the centre and the provinces.[16] There was, however, no evidence that such innovations achieved any markedly improved communication between the leadership and ordinary citizens: the Jiu Valley unrest of 1977 does not appear to have been anticipated, and Ceauşescu's response to the Polish crisis in 1980 (see below) seemed to indicate anxiety about a possible new outbreak of unrest inside Romania.

In Czechoslovakia, the attempt was made in 1968 to achieve a real democratization within the communist party (for example, by allowing local party organizations to propose candidates for election, in place of the practice of electing candidates nominated by the Politburo and Central Committee and also by allowing a minority within the party publicly to defend its position). The Prague reformers also envisaged a pluralization of political life, with non-communist groups able to assert influence. But the reform experiment was too short-lived to allow confident conclusions to be drawn about the workability of these ideas, either in Czechoslovakia or in other socialist states. 1968 was in fact to prove a watershed for development within all the bloc states, in the negative sense that it largely put an end to hopes that the political systems could be radically reformed from within: as from that year, revisionism was dead. As well as affecting attitudes inside the ruling parties, this also had an important effect on the attitudes and methods of the non-party critics and opposition: the approach adopted by KOR in Poland for example was that impetus for change was likely to come, not from within the PUWP, but from sustained pressure from social groups acting independently of the party.

It was in Poland that the issues of participation, communication and democratization acquired the most sustained relevance. In 1956 there were high hopes that party methods would change at least to the extent of permitting greater participation from below in the formulation of policy. At the same time it was hoped that newly formed 'workers' councils' would provide substantial worker participation in economic decision-making. Both hopes were quickly dashed: the party soon reasserted its authoritarian habits, and workers' councils were subsumed into 'conferences of workers' self-management' with an actual bias towards management.[17] In the 1970 crisis, the same basic issues surfaced again. Suggestions were put forward for limited tenure to be attached to the top party offices and for a degree of rotation of office-holders. Failure of communication between the party leadership and grass-roots opinion, including the rioting of Gdansk workers, 40 per cent of whom held party cards, was singled out for remedial action. Gierek introduced a new approach epitomized in his (1971) exchange with shipyard workers: 'Will you help me?' Response: 'We will!' Yet in 1976, and again still more strikingly in 1980, precisely the same problem surfaced again. Mieczyslaw Rakowski, editor of *Polityka*, pinpointed the fundamental problem when he observed that 'a feedback should exist between the authorities and society'.[18] The historic significance of the Gdansk agreement in 1980, as perceived by another *Polytika* writer,[19] was that the PUWP acknowledged for the first time that 'neither the Party itself nor the organizations and bodies directed by it are the sole representatives of society'. Less clear, as will be discussed later, was the way towards breaking down what was seen by reform-minded communists as the failures in democracy and free expression within the party itself. At one and the same time, calls were heard for the strengthening of Leninist and democratic-centralist methods, and for devising means to prevent the all-too-familiar situation in which party members had in practice hidden their real views out of loyalty (or sycophancy) to its leader.

3 The development of Soviet policy towards Eastern Europe

The development of Soviet policy towards Eastern Europe can be separated into five main phases: the Stalinist phase from 1944-53; a post-Stalinist period of uncertainty from 1953-8; the period of Khrushchev's clear ascendancy in 1958-64; the phase of the consolidation of power by Leonid Brezhnev in 1964-8; and finally the mature period of Brezhnev's leadership from 1968 until the time of writing.

The Stalin and Khrushchev eras

The Stalinist phase was the least complex. Stalin saw Eastern Europe as a highly valuable buffer-zone whose acquisition by the Soviet Union would serve as a guarantee against the repetition of the traumatic experience of Hitler's lightning offensive against the Soviet Union in 1941-2. He also evidently saw the area as a useful springboard for extending communist influence into Western Europe, although events were to prove this hope forlorn: the ideological advantage passed quickly to the West. At the same time the Soviet Union viewed the East European states as a source of economic benefit: while the ex-enemy territories of East Germany, Romania and Hungary were made to pay the greatest tribute, all the bloc states were compelled to contribute heavily to Soviet needs. A striking example was the export of huge quantities of Polish coal to the Soviet Union at what was for the latter a highly advantageous price. The extent of Soviet exploitation of Eastern Europe has been estimated as a total of $20 billion in the 1945-56 period.[1]

The effect of the uncertainties engendered in the Soviet Union in the years immediately following Stalin's death has been briefly described in the preceding chapter. Khrushchev's emergence as undisputed leader, which was not confirmed until 1958 with the final defeat of the 'anti-party group' of Molotov, Malenkov and Kaganovich, resulted in a somewhat less unequal relationship between the Soviet Union and the East European states. Until 1958 the Soviet leadership was without a consistent strategy and the East Europeans were left to interpret the implications for them of the retreat from Stalinism as best they could. The uncertainty of Soviet policy in Poland is illustrated in the events surrounding Khrushchev's sudden trip to Warsaw in October 1956 — together with Marshal Konev and Mikoyan — and`his attendance at the crucial meeting of the Polish Central Committee at which Gomulka was elected. The evidence (including Khrushchev's own account) shows that while Khrushchev was prepared to allow the Polish Central Committee some latitude in resolving the crisis of confidence in the Polish leadership in its own way, his attitude was also heavily influenced by what he described as a wave of feeling in Poland of a 'dangerously anti-Soviet character'.[2] He was less than entirely happy about the Poles' preference for Gomulka as new party leader, though he later came to accept that Gomulka was at least not ill-disposed towards the Soviet Union. The use of Soviet troops to arrest what were regarded as counter-revolutionary forces was only narrowly averted when it became evident, amongst other things, that Polish security units were under orders to block the roads giving access to Warsaw. Had Soviet troops marched into Warsaw, as was planned but countermanded by Khrushchev after an impassioned plea by Gomulka, there would certainly have been bloodshed, and the restoration of friendship between the two nations would have been a formidable task.

The groping nature of Soviet policy-making at this time, and its relative openness, is also illustrated by the account in the recently published diaries of the former Yugoslav Ambassador to Moscow, Veljko Mićunović of Khrushchev's secret visit to Tito, on the island of Brioni on the eve of the fateful decision to mount a military intervention in Hungary in October 1956.[3] Khrushchev's aim was to secure Tito's moral support for the intervention (in which he was successful) and also to obtain the Yugoslav leader's advice on the choice of a new First Secretary of the Hungarian Communist Party. When Khrushchev indicated that the Soviet preference was for Ferenc Munnich, the former Hungarian Ambassador to Moscow, Tito pointed out that in the circumstances the Moscow connection would hardly be an asset; he recommended instead János Kádár as a leader likely to command broad popular support. Khrushchev was now slow to grasp the point and the advice was readily accepted. The co-operation between Khrushchev and Tito was destroyed not long afterwards when, contrary to Yugoslav hopes, the Soviet government decided to endorse the call for the execution of Imre Nagy. Nevertheless, President Tito could claim to have had an important influence in helping to promote the national reconciliation in Hungary which has been so closely connected with the personality of Kádár.

Soviet flexibility at this time was also reflected in the decision taken in 1958 to withdraw Soviet armed forces from Romania. According to the account in Khrushchev's memoirs,[4] the Romanians had first requested the withdrawal of Soviet forces in 1953 when, during a visit to Moscow by General Bodnăraş, the latter had argued that a Soviet presence was unnecessary since Romania had no hostile states on her borders. Khrushchev had countered at the time that the propinquity of Turkey was sufficient threat, but had later adopted a different view when he set his heart on achieving major reductions in Soviet military manpower. While Soviet military planners have consistently set much higher strategic store by the 'northern tier' of Poland, East Germany and Czechoslovakia than they have by the southern East European countries, the presence of Soviet forces in a bloc country has obvious political significance in the context of internal security and overall Soviet leverage. Khrushchev would seem to have paid surprisingly little regard to the latter aspect, although it is true that few in 1958 would have predicted the degree to which Romania was later to develop an independent stance in the conduct of its external affairs.

1958 was above all important as the year in which Khrushchev consolidated his personal power. In the following years of his leadership he adopted a more vigorous and adventurous international posture; concern about Eastern Europe gave way to growing preoccupation with developments in the outside world, including the escalating quarrel with China and rivalry with the United States. The Soviet Union evinced greater interest in and support for national liberation movements and began to play a more active role in Asia, the Middle East and Africa, while in the Americas the Cuban missile affair (1962) marked the boldest Soviet foray so far witnessed in the confrontation with the United States. In Eastern Europe, Khrushchev's main concerns were to consolidate the new post-Stalin order and to achieve a measure of economic integration through the strengthening of the hitherto flimsy Comecon structure. In part, this latter concern was a response to the moves towards West European unity in the wake of the Rome Treaty. The Soviet desire to introduce a system of supranational planning marked a significant departure from Stalinist methods of control with their emphasis on strictly bilateral links between the Soviet Union and the other fraternal states. Not surprisingly, however, many East Europeans feared that the development of planning on a multilateral basis would in practice allow the Soviet Union to play a yet more preponderant role in bloc affairs. Khrushchev's proclaimed belief that the socialist states would enter the stage of full communism 'simultaneously' appeared to imply the pursuit of a degree of uniformity which might threaten such experiments as the 'Polish way' to socialism. In the event, Khrushchev's aim of achieving economic integration on the basis of supranational planning was thwarted by Romanian obstructionism.

The dispute with China, which came into the open in 1960, complicated Khrushchev's task in Eastern Europe. Almost equally awkward was the emergence in Western Europe of the 'polycentric' vision of the world communist movement, developed by the Italian communist leader, Togliatti. The fissures in the communist movement appeared to offer opportunities to Gomulka in Poland, who was acutely conscious of the weak ideological basis for the Polish road to socialism as viewed by ideologists in Moscow,[5] and who was anxious (in his first years of power) to try to maintain and, if possible, enlarge his freedom of manoeuvre. In the event, China was to prove of little use to him: the Chinese leadership was critical of the course of internal developments in Poland which in its view smacked of revisionist deviation. Gomulka, who for a time adopted an intermediary position between the two protagonists, in the end felt compelled to come down firmly on the Soviet side, particularly after the Chinese launched strong attacks against Yugoslavia. The growth of polycentrism, on the other hand, proved to be of indisputable benefit to those seeking to maintain Poland's margin of autonomy: this concept could be invoked both to justify Poland's unorthodox agricultural policy together with the *modus vivendi* with the Church and to support the development of economic, cultural and other links with the West in line with Poland's cultural heritage.

It was the exploitation by Romania of the Sino–Soviet dispute which caused Khrushchev the greatest problems. In 1962-3, Gheorghiu-Dej, aided by his adroit foreign minister, Maurer, attempted to mediate between the Soviet and Chinese leaderships as a way of demonstrating Romania's capacity for independent action in the international realm, and in order to develop a margin of manoeuvrability *vis-à-vis* the USSR. The attempt ended in failure. But the Romanian leadership was determined to preserve a degree of independence within the socialist commonwealth notwithstanding this setback. Essentially a defensive measure, the Romanian 'Declaration of Independence' of April 1964 laid the theoretical basis for the international policy which Romania has been pursuing to this day. The Declaration laid emphasis on the principles of national independence, sovereignty, equal rights, mutually advantageous comradely assistance, non-interference in internal affairs, observance of territorial integrity and the principles of socialist internationalism. Most significantly, it claimed that 'it is the sovereign right of each socialist state to elaborate, choose or change the forms and methods of socialist construction'. It also claimed, with obvious reference to the role of the Soviet Union, that 'no specific and individual interests can be presented as general interests, as objective requirements of the development of the socialist system.[6] The essence of the Romanian position, as Kenneth Jowitt has rightly observed, was that relations between ruling communist parties and governments should be on a co-operative basis, with a right of dissent and non-participation, rather than on the principle that all decisions be taken unanimously.[7] Romania has managed to uphold this position up to the present times, notwithstanding continuing efforts by the Soviet Union to promote the unanimity principle.

The Brezhnev/Kosygin leadership, which succeeded that of Khrushchev in the autumn of 1964, approached the problems of international relations with more modest objectives and with a greater sense of realism about the limits of Soviet power. A major factor in Khrushchev's demise had been his Cuban policy in 1962-3 which, apart from the fearsome risks of a nuclear exchange which it had carried, culminated in by far the most serious diplomatic reverse suffered by the Soviet Union after World War II. The new Soviet leadership was concerned to reduce the gap between aspiration and reality by building up the strength of the Soviet armed forces: this they proceeded patiently to do as part of a long-term process of repairing Soviet prestige. Meanwhile dramatic foreign policy initiatives were eschewed. Until 1968, Brezhnev's domestic power-base was less than fully secure, and domestic preoccupations loomed large. In Eastern Europe, the accent was on consolidation of the alliance and especially its military arm, the Warsaw Pact.

The process of strengthening the armed forces of the East European states was begun by Khrushchev in the early 1960s. The East European forces were supplied with more modern weapons (including MIG-21 and SU 7 aircraft and T-54 and T-55 tanks). Multilateral training exercises of the Warsaw Pact forces began to be held, and by the mid-1960s could be described as serious combat-training activities. The Brezhnev leadership decided at an early stage to supplement the military content of the WTO by developing it as an instrument of political as well as military co-ordination. In September 1965 Brezhnev underlined the need for 'further perfecting the Warsaw Treaty Organization' and declared that a 'permanent and prompt mechanism for considering pressing problems' was required within its framework.

In the event, Brezhnev's call for the strengthening of the institutional framework of the Warsaw Pact fared no better than Khrushchev's attempt to make Comecon into a supranational organ. As in the latter case, the Soviet position appears to have been weakened above all by the activities of the Romanians: in May 1966, just two months before the important Bucharest conference of the Political Consultative Committee (PCC) of the Warsaw Pact, Romania is reported to have put forward radical proposals for the revamping of the Pact's military organization, the effect of which would have been to reduce Soviet predominance and commensurately increase the influence of the East Europeans within it.[8] The Romanian proposals apparently included, as well as a call for the rotation of the post of Commander-in-Chief, a proposal that Soviet forces were no longer necessary in Eastern Europe, apart from in East Germany, and that any country that wanted such troops should bear the cost itself. At the same time Ceauşescu (in a speech of 7 May 1966) made a number of anti-Russian remarks and issued a thinly veiled call for the dissolution of military blocs. Although the Romanian position did not directly conflict with the Soviet proposal for a strengthening of the *political* mechanism of the alliance, the Romanian attitude was clearly unfavourable to any form of increased co-ordination which would have given greater effective control to the Soviet Union. At its July meeting, the PCC was unable to register progress towards either the Soviet or the Romanian goals. Although there is no direct evidence of this, it seems probable that some others in the bloc apart from Romania joined in frustrating the Soviet proposal; it is at least clear from later evidence that the Czechs shared Romanian attitudes on a number of points,[9] and it seems likely that other East Europeans too shared some of them.

The Brezhnev leadership

In its first four years, the Brezhnev leadership was cautious and some-what ambivalent in the conduct of international diplomacy. The Soviet leaders appear to have entertained some hope that they might be able to exploit American embroilment in Vietnam by courting better relations with West European countries to the exclusion of the United States. France was seemingly viewed in this light. The Soviet leaders were attracted by the prospects of increased trade with European countries, especially the Federal Republic of Germany, not least as a source of advanced technology for which there were no local substitutes. On the other hand, the leadership was afraid that any general relaxation of tension in Europe would carry greater risks than benefits if it were not preceded by a resolution of the German problem in a way in which would ensure international recognition of the German Democratic Republic. They were distrustful both of the early *Ostpolitik* of the Brandt–Kiesinger coalition and of the United States government's call for 'building bridges' between East and West. In the communiqué issued at the end of the Bucharest meeting of the PCC (1966), the Warsaw Pact states called for an 'all-European conference to discuss security and promote European co-operation', The communiqué also echoed a Romanian idea by proposing the liquidation of military alliances (albeit in the safe knowledge that this would be unacceptable to NATO). But by far the most pressing Soviet concerns were reflected in the communiqué's call for a solution to the German problem on the basis of acceptance of the 'reality' of two German states, and the demand that the Federal Republic should be denied access to nuclear weapons in any form.

In short, the Soviet Union showed increasing interest during the 1960s in a relaxation of tension in Europe, both as a means of strengthening its overall strategic and political position in the continent and as a means of obtaining direct benefit for its economy. But this was balanced by still strong fears, particularly about the intentions of the FRG, whose policies proved to be a crucial determinant in the eventual denoument. The ambivalence in the 1960s to the development of the East European states' relations with the West (discussed later) must be seen in this context.

The 1968 invasion of Czechoslovakia by the Soviet Union and four other Warsaw Pact states served as a catalyst in the development of Soviet policy in Europe. In 1966-8, the Brezhnev leadership was much exercised by the fear that its hold over Eastern Europe might be undermined as a result of Bonn's more assertive policies in this area, supported by a hostile United States. By the end of 1967, Bonn had established trade offices in four East European states, and the establishment of diplomatic relations with Romania in January 1967 was seen by the Soviet Union as a potentially dangerous development. The possibility that Czechoslovakia might be sucked into the West German sphere of influence was one of the considerations which evidently influenced the Kremlin in deciding its policy towards the Dubček leadership.[10] At the same time there were certainly some within the Soviet Politburo who could already see that the evolution of West German policy presented opportunities as well as risks, and that Bonn's professed interest in developing better relations with its East European neighbours could, in the right circumstances, be turned to Soviet advantage in consolidating the post-war territorial and political status quo in Eastern Europe. What from the Soviet point of view was unfortunate in the situation as it was developing in the period preceding the invasion of Czechoslovakia was that divisive trends in Eastern Europe were becoming so marked that there seemed a real threat to the Soviet Union's ability to co-ordinate the international policies of the socialist community. Unless checked, this could even lead to Western states entertaining hopes of presiding over the dismemberment of the Soviet empire.

The invasion of Czechoslovakia, and the subsequent 'normalization', provided the opportunity to stabilize the situation in Eastern Europe and to arrest the risk of disintegration. The enunciation in 1968 of the 'Brezhnev Doctrine' reaffirmed, in much more explicit terms than previously, the principle that the states of the socialist community are governed by 'common laws', deviation from which may call for 'fraternal' corrective action.[11] Although Romania dissociated itself from the Czech intervention and made it clear that it did not subscribe to the Doctrine, the Soviet Union had given unmistakable proof of its readiness to employ force if it judged its essential interests to be threatened. Notwithstanding the damage suffered by the Soviet image in the West, the Soviet leadership, greatly strengthened by the belief that it had reasserted control within its fief, and encouraged by Herr Brandt's election victory in August 1969, took up the challenge of Bonn's *Ostpolitik*. At Warsaw Pact meetings in October and December 1969, new proposals were put forward for the holding of an All-European Security Conference. In December the Soviet Union also engaged in bilateral talks with the new Brandt government. These moves were to lead to the normalization of relations between the FRG and the Soviet Union, to be followed shortly by Polish-FRG normalization in the course of 1970. A four-power agreement on Berlin, concluded in 1971, was the final step in preparing the way for the opening in Helsinki in 1972 of talks on the holding of a Conference of Security and Co-operation in Europe which were to culminate - in 1975 - in the signature of the Helsinki Final Act. The latter document, although not a peace treaty, was viewed by the Brezhnev leadership as the vindication of Soviet efforts to gain general confirmation of the post-war territorial and political status quo. It was also significant – though, naturally enough, the Kremlin did not concede this – as an attempt to codify détente in a way which went some way beyond the basic Soviet conception (normalization of relations between states for mutual economic and security benefit) to include such concepts as increased contacts between people and individuals, human rights, and full respect for national sovereignty.

Meanwhile, within the East European alliance, the Brezhnev leadership tried to give further practical content to the concept of camp solidarity by promoting integration in the political, military and economic spheres. The two major achievements were the reform of the military structure of the Warsaw Pact in a manner which went some way towards meeting East European concerns without conceding the more radical demands of the Romanians, and the elaboration of a Comprehensive Programme of Integration (1971) within Comecon along Soviet-approved lines. In the WTO, the new system established in 1969 allowed East European officers of Major-General's rank to act as deputy chiefs of staff in a newly constituted permanent staff of the Pact armed forces. It also reconstituted the Joint Command in a way which was more acceptable to East European sensitivities. The main result of the important

Comecon Comprehensive Programme was to give impetus to co-ordinated long-term planning and to the elaboration of joint projects, especially in the fields of energy and transport. The method of integration – by state-to-state agreement, rather than the introduction of market mechanisms favoured by Hungarian and some other East European planners – was fully to Soviet taste: it ensured that economic would remain subordinate to political considerations, and that the fact of Soviet preponderance within the bloc would find due reflection in the process of economic integration.

The area in which the Brezhnev policies have been least successful is probably that of political co-ordination. The Warsaw Pact still has no permanent political secretariat comparable to NATO's and no more has been heard of the 1965 Brezhnev proposal for a permanent political organ of this kind. However, the Political Consultative Committee (established in 1961) has met more frequently since 1968 (roughly once a year in contrast to the irregular meetings previously) and the co-ordination of positions which was required for the successful conclusion of the CSCE negotiations may be reckoned by the Russians to have helped to foster the habit of close consulation at working as well as higher levels (in much the same way as co-ordination of CSCE policy amongst EEC states is claimed to have strengthened the political co-operation process of the Nine).

Policy in the 1980s

At the opening of the 1980s, the Brezhnev leadership faces some of the same problems, in its management of the bloc, as it did in 1968. Romania continues to pursue a relatively independent foreign policy, as evidenced in its critical stance regarding the Soviet invasion of Afghanistan and – at another level – the conclusion in 1980 of a special arrangement with the EEC: In Poland in 1980, as in Czechoslovakia in 1968, spontaneous forces appeared to threaten the control of the communist party and hence to threaten Poland's reliability as a member of the Warsaw Pact. The international environment has however altered perceptibly in the intervening years, partly as a result of the carefully conceived policies of the Brezhnev leadership in its second phase. Whereas in 1968 détente had not yet taken firm root and at least an influential part of the Soviet leadership was still preoccupied with the fear that West Germany threatened the East European status quo, the developments of the first half of the 1970s strengthened Soviet perceptions of the benefits of practical co-operation with the West and allayed Soviet anxieties about the permanence of the territorial and political status quo in Europe.

At the end of the 1970s, the Soviet leaders became increasingly concerned about the direction of US policies, and were disappointed by the failure of the US Congress in 1979-80 to ratify the SALT-2 agreement. The NATO decision to modernize theatre nuclear forces in Europe in November 1979, and the strong US reaction to the Soviet intervention in Afghanistan in the following month, gave the Kremlin cause to question some of the premises on which the détente policies of the 1970s were based. None the less, there was no sign of any marked diminution in Soviet interest in cultivating closer relations with the countries of Western Europe, not least as a means of continuing to import advanced technology and capital equipment. This factor, as will be analysed later, serves both to increase Soviet interest in achieving the co-ordination of bloc policies on what it sees as vital international issues, and permits East European governments to continue to develop links with the West to the extent they deem prudent for their own viability.

Methods of control

The Soviet Union maintains its hegemony in Eastern Europe by a variety of means, including ideological control, influence in the selection of communist party leaders in bloc states, bilateral and multilateral meetings between Soviet and bloc leaders, and normal diplomatic activity. Although this is poorly documented, an important instrument for monitoring developments in the bloc is the KGB, which co-ordinates the activities of all the bloc security services and which is heavily represented within these. Not altogether surprisingly, the available detailed evidence about the manner in which these instruments are used is sketchy. The best evidence tends to come from what has been learnt from past crises, such as those of 1956 in Hungary and 1968 in Czechoslovakia. It is evident that the direct controls of the Stalinist era have been largely replaced by levers of an informal, and sometimes improvised, kind. The recent history of Soviet relations with the three countries which are the subject of this study also demonstrates that there have been substantial differences in the degree of Soviet influence, and in the manner in which it has been exerted, as between different bloc states. In all of the bloc states, the Soviet leaders have relied heavily on the cultivation of close personal relations with their bloc counterparts, with a view to ensuring that the leaders of East European states are worthy of confidence, both in terms of their loyalty to the Soviet Union and of their ability to maintain control of their respective populaces. Brezhnev's meetings with First Secretaries of bloc parties in the Crimea in August of each year have been one manifestation of this. Soviet interest in leadership changes, and reactions to recent bloc crises, are examined in later chapters.

The Soviet Union is at the same time able to extend its influence by a vast web of contacts between party and government officials, managers, scientists, journalists, writers, historians, artists, etc. It is beyond the scope of this overview to describe in detail these more or less regularized links, but it is worth noting their institutionalization in the 'friendship' treaties, allying the East European states with the Soviet Union and with each other. An important element is the regular meetings between party officials dealing with ideological matters. The Romanians have participated fully in these, although sometimes registering dissent from such Soviet-favoured concepts as 'proletarian internationalism'. Meetings of journalists are also an important factor in co-ordination.

Essential Soviet concerns

What have been the basic constant factors affecting the Soviet attitude to Eastern Europe? Has the emphasis altered?

The most elemental and deeply rooted Soviet concern is about security: in the Soviet mind today, as in the 1940s, Eastern Europe represents a highly valuable extension of its frontiers. While developments in the field of nuclear warfare may have marginally reduced the strategic importance of the area, all the evidence indicates that the Soviet government continues to attach tremendous importance to the maintenance of its position, especially in the three northern tier countries-East Germany, Czechoslovakia and Poland. The psychological importance of this is well illustrated in Mlynar's first-hand account of the meeting in August 1968 in Moscow between the Soviet and Czech Politburos. In explaining the Soviet invasion, Brezhnev spoke emotionally about the immense significance for Czechoslovakia as well as for the Soviet Union of the great sacrifices made by Soviet soldiers during the war, and of the need to preserve the guarantee of security which the post-war borders represented. It was, he asserted, to preserve these 'common borders' that the fateful decision to intervene had been taken. [12]

The second major Soviet concern is ideological: the countries of Eastern Europe constitute an important part of what Soviet ideologists call the 'world socialist system'. The secession of any of these states would represent a serious reverse to the cause of world socialism. [13] One effect of the Sino-Soviet dispute has been to increase still further the interest of the Soviet Union in maintaining ideological orthodoxy amongst the countries which remain loyal to the Soviet brand of socialism. This is partly because the Soviet Union needs as many allies as it can muster in its various attempts to isolate the Chinese in the world communist movement. Still more fundamental is the importance of ideology as the buttress of the political system in the Soviet Union and as the source of authority of its rulers. Clearly, not all Soviet decisions are inspired by ideology as such. Agreement to enter negotiations on nuclear non-proliferation or strategic arms limitation talks has less to do with tenets of Marxism–Leninism than with a perceived need to avert nuclear destruction: as the Kremlin has itself tellingly recognized, the nuclear bomb is not subject to the rules of class war. However, the validating function of ideology is of real importance: the Soviet leaders need to be able to show that the principles of Marxism–Leninism on which their political system is based are of universal validity. The fact that the Soviet interpretation of these principles has been so severely challenged in the last two decades makes it still more imperative from the Soviet viewpoint to demonstrate that their interpretation enjoys successful application at least in Eastern Europe. The reverse side of the coin is that the development within Eastern Europe of any new model of socialism which challenges Marxist–Leninist ideology as interpreted by the Soviet Union is perceived as a threat to the authority of the CPSU leadership within the Soviet Union itself. Although the perception of such a risk is unlikely to have been the sole reason for the Soviet decision to invade Czechoslovakia in 1968, it may well have been the decisive factor.[14]

A parallel Soviet concern has been to maintain a predominant influence in the interpretation of communist ideology as a means of asserting its influence over Eastern Europe, and of maintaining the cohesion of the socialist camp. The debate in the communist movement in the late 1950s about the role of the Communist Party of the Soviet Union (CPSU) was significant, mainly in terms of its implications for the practical limits of Soviet control. Gomulka's refusal at this time formally to accord a directing role in the movement to the CPSU reflected his determination to preserve substantial leeway to apply Polish remedies to Polish problems. Romania's challenge to the Soviet Union in the 1960s and 1970s was similarly motivated by a desire to pursue its own national economic and foreign policies. The CPSU has shown some ideological flexibility in accommodating these challenges. However, this flexibility has not extended to the concepts of democratic centralism and the leading role of the communist party. The reasons for this are threefold. First, the maintenance of control by a tightly-knit communist party, whose leadership is not elected by local party organizations but selected on the basis of nominations by the Central Committee, provides a tested means of holding power and of countering attempted subversion or counter-revolution. Second, this tight method of control allows the Soviet Union to keep watch over developments through personal links with a relatively small number of highly placed individuals in East European parties, and an opportunity to assert its interests through the actual process of selection of new leaderships. Third, the maintenance of a uniform system of party control which is essentially authoritarian facilitates the task of co-ordinating the policies of bloc states on what are considered by the Soviet Union to be vital issues of security and ideological conformity in the face of external challenges.[15] It was hardly surprising that the flirtation of Czechoslovak reformers in 1968 with the idea that the communist party should play a 'guiding' rather than a directing role aroused acute misgivings in Moscow.

Scholars have devoted much time to questioning whether ideological considerations, or considerations of Soviet national self-interest, are uppermost in the minds of Soviet policy-makers. This question may often be more academic than real. In the case of policy towards Eastern Europe, Soviet national interests, as defined primarily in terms of security, and Soviet ideological concerns are very closely intertwined. Rightly or wrongly, Soviet leaders have appeared to believe that ideological conformity is an essential ingredient in maintaining an organic relationship with the states of Eastern Europe. This organic relationship is in turn the guarantee of the security of the Soviet Union, as expressed in Brezhnev's above-quoted justification to Dubček for the invasion of Czechoslovakia. Concern for the 'borders of socialism' and concern for ideological orthodoxy are to a large extent fused in Soviet thinking. Kovalev's comment about the lamentable effects of the weakening of any link in the world socialist system can be read interchangeably in terms of either ideological purity or defensive strength.

The third major Soviet concern in Eastern Europe is economic. Eastern Europe is useful to the Soviet Union as an assured and relatively 'soft' market for a variety of industrial products, including engineering products and consumer goods, which it would be much more difficult to sell in outside markets. The East European states obtain most of their requirements for imported raw materials from the USSR and have assisted the latter by participating in massive investment projects related to the extraction of natural resources, such as the Orenburg pipeline. In general, the advantage to the Soviet Union of selling raw materials to Eastern Europe is distinctly less than that of selling finished products, since Soviet raw materials are much more easily marketable than finished products in the West, for hard currency. In the last decade, the Russians have sold oil to the East Europeans at prices which are substantially below world prices: according to Soviet sources, the saving to Eastern Europe in 1976-80 was in the order of 5,000 million roubles or US $7,000 million at the official (valuta roubles) exchange rate. It has been persuasively argued that during the 1970s Eastern Europe became a net economic liability to the Soviet Union.[16] If, however, the political benefits the USSR can expect to gain in terms of increased East European dependence are added to the balance sheet, the assessment of net advantage to the Soviet Union is bound to be more positive. There is also a psychological factor affecting Soviet planners: the centrally planned nature of the East European economies and the possibilities for establishing trading and investment patterns over a long timescale make Eastern Europe particularly attractive to Soviet planners. The relative stability and reliability of these markets is seen to contrast favourably with the vicissitudes besetting Soviet trade with the Western world. Whatever, the precise balance of costs and benefits, it can safely be concluded that in recent years the economic aspects of Soviet–East European relations are likely to have been viewed by the Russians as of less benefit than the strategic and ideological aspects which have been discussed.

There are a number of other ways in which Eastern Europe provides benefits to the Soviet Union. Although the bloc countries spend substantially less of their national income on defence than does the USSR, their armed forces usefully augment the Soviet Union's defensive shield. It is beyond the scope of this study to assess the degree of this usefulness, which has been the subject of debate amongst analysts. Some have queried the reliability of forces of some East European states in the event of Soviet offensive operations in Europe. It seems in fact likely that the Soviet Union would in such circumstances rely heavily on its own armed forces, with East European units being allotted secondary roles (which could however include some limited offensive, in addition to defensive, functions). Eastern Europe is also of some value as a producer of a range of items of military equipment. It is nevertheless unlikely that Soviet strategists would regard Eastern Europe's direct military contribution as comparable to the considerable benefit to be derived from the simple fact of the extension of frontiers which flows from the Warsaw Alliance.

Another benefit the Soviet Union derives from Eastern Europe is in offering active material as well as moral support for Soviet objectives in the Third World, including contributing to the success of national liberation movements. Examples are the ever-increasing activities of the German Democratic Republic in Africa, and the large Czechoslovak aid programmes to Third-World countries which are of political interest to the Soviet Union. The bloc intelligence services make a substantial contribution to the furtherance of Soviet objectives outside as well as within the bloc. The allegiance of Eastern Europe must also be welcome to the Soviet leaders in many more commonplace ways: for example, as a conveniently close area for foreign travel and tourism which is free from ideological contamination (although there may be exceptions to the rule, such as Czechoslovakia in 1968 and Poland in 1980 and the scale of these contacts is in any case rather small). However, in the overall balance sheet, there seems little doubt that national security and ideological reinforcement are the overriding Soviet concerns in the area.

Change of emphasis

It may be concluded that there has been an evolution in the post-war years of the methods of Soviet control in Eastern Europe, with direct controls giving way to indirect and informal forms of influence. Greater weight continues to be given to bilateral than to multilateral mechanisms of co-ordination, the attempt by Khrushchev to introduce supranational economic planning having come to nothing. Since 1968, the Brezhnev Doctrine has established ground rules which, if still not without some ambiguity, have made it plain that the maintenance of the leading role of the communist party in a bloc state is the minimal condition of necessary conformity. Although periodically embarrassed by Romanian activities since the early 1960s, the Soviet Union has been relatively successful in achieving co-ordination of foreign policy amongst bloc states, for instance in the CSCE negotiations of 1972-5.

If in the post-Stalin era the Central Soviet practical objective is seen to be the achievement of a combination of cohesion and viability, the post-1968 Brezhnev era can show some successes. The reforms of the Warsaw Pact of 1969 provided evidence of a Soviet desire to accommodate its allies, even if this affected form more than substance. While the 1971 Comprehensive Programme of Integration was in many respects a success for the Soviet viewpoint in contrast to those of the more innovative economic thinkers in Eastern Europe, the preservation, at Romanian insistence, of the unanimity principle has preserved the option of non-participation for the East European states. In successive Polish crises, the Soviet Union has behaved circumspectly and with sensitivity to the peculiarities of Polish conditions. The CSCE process and the pursuit of détente have given the East European states greater leeway to develop ties with Western Europe in line with their historical and cultural traditions, while for the Soviet Union the Final Act provided useful recognition of the post-war frontiers in Eastern Europe. Viewed from the Soviet angle, the negative side of the picture is that closer Western connections have in some respects militated against the objective of cohesion on which the Soviet leadership placed such stress in 1968. The Polish crisis of 1980, in which the authority of the communist party was at stake, was influenced by the effects of the relaxation of tension in Europe. This crisis represented probably the most serious challenge which the Soviet Union has had to face in Eastern Europe since the war; its implications, and those of other recent manifestations of unrest in the sub-region, are the subject of later treatment.

Subordination or alliance?

Even this brief description has served to highlight a number of fairly radical differences between the Eastern and Western alliance systems and in economic integration arrangements. In the latter sphere, the process of integration in Comecon has so far produced somewhat disappointing results, and has not matched the degree of genuine co-operation achieved by the EEC. But its general drift has reflected Soviet to a much greater degree than East European concerns; this subject is discussed further in Chapter 6.

In the military sphere, while the Warsaw Treaty has come to include some of the trappings of a collaborative alliance as opposed to a system of subordination, it is hard to resist the conclusion that it more resembles the latter. The continuing absence of a regular mechanism for political consultation, comparable to the NATO Council and the NATO Political Committee, is but one aspect of this.

Although one may conceive of a theoretical model in which the Soviet Union would treat the East European states in something like the manner of its relationship with Finland (that is, allowing freedom to operate a non-communist political system provided certain minimal Soviet desiderata in the field of security and foreign policy are met), there has been no sign of Soviet thinking moving in such a direction. The essence of the Brezhnev Doctrine, which has been the cornerstone of Soviet policy towards Eastern Europe since 1968, is that the states of the socialist community are bound together organically, not least by ideological bonds. The key element in this is the maintenance of the leading role of the communist party in each bloc state.

The efficacy of the ideological cement uniting the 'socialist commonwealth' can easily be exaggerated. But there is nothing to suggest that the Soviet leaders are becoming any less disposed to use ideology as a means of promoting Soviet national goals. The clear tenor of Soviet ideological manuals[17] is that what is good for the Soviet Union is good for the camp as a whole. This is what in effect is meant by such pronouncements of the ideologues as: 'The practice of socialist construction and the entire experience of the world socialist system has shown that the correctly interpreted national interests of the individual country cannot fail to coincide with the internationalist interests of the entire socialist system.'[18] The USSR is seen as the interpreter of the common laws of socialist development, although naturally enough this is never spelt out in so many words.

Whether or not the Soviet Union sees the East European states as nation-states in the sense generally understood in the West is a subject on which one can only speculate. Interestingly, Brezhnev at the Twenty-fifth Party Congress (1976) spoke of a deepening rapprochement between the socialist states. The Russian word used (*sblizhenie*) is the word used for the first stage of the merger of the Socialist Republics in the Soviet Union itself — the final stage being 'fusion' (*slianie*). Also significantly, however, at the Twenty-sixth Party Congress (1981) Brezhnev referred to the same concept in notably more defensive terms. He stated that rapprochement 'continues to develop', but qualified this by saying that it did not blot out the national characteristics of each of the socialist countries; and that there existed 'a wealth of ways and methods of developing the socialist way of life'. Yugoslav commentators saw this as a positive sign of a slightly greater Soviet disposition to tolerate diversity.

It may be concluded that Soviet leaders would appear to have come to acknowledge that, in a practical perspective, the process of integration of the socialist commonwealth must be tackled gradually and with caution. Nevertheless, the basic strand of Soviet thinking is that the socialist commonwealth is *organically* interrelated and that the Soviet Union plays the key and guiding role in co-ordinating its development along roughly common lines.

4 The opening to the exterior

Eastern Europe's opening to the West dates from the mid-1950s and was closely connected with the momentous changes in Soviet policies adumbrated in Khrushchev's Twentieth Party Congress speech. 1956 was the key year in three senses. The suppression of the Hungarian uprising demonstrated to those in Eastern Europe who hoped for salvation through liberation by the West that such hopes were entirely illusory. The corollary was that the West did not represent a direct threat to the East European regimes, although there remained unease about the possible consequences of the re-armament of the Federal Republic of Germany. Second, Soviet acknowledgement of 'separate paths to social-ism' implied some recognition that the minimum necessary respect for local peculiarities would be tolerated, although this must be within the context of strictly defined general laws of socialist construction. This was taken by East Europeans to pertain to East European cultural links with the West as well as other aspects of the 'national particular', in the Marxist-Leninist jargon. Third, the events in Hungary and Poland convinced a number of East European communists that it was no longer sufficient to look to the Moscow connection as a sure guarantee: if the fate of a Rákosi or a Berman was to be avoided, it was necessary to learn to stand on one's own feet. The crucially important later land-mark came in 1970 with the normalization of relations between the Federal Republic of Germany and the Soviet Union and Poland, and the emergence of a new US-Soviet relationship in the 1970s. Until 1969, when Herr Brandt formed a coalition with the FDP, there were many East European, as well as Soviet, communists who feared that FRG policies, in conjunction with those of the US, might yet undermine the existing political order and status quo in Eastern Europe. The reassurance provided by the *Ostpolitik* of the Brandt government was complemented by the commitment of the incoming Nixon administration in 1969 to a policy of détente which eschewed the exploitation of Soviet difficulties in Eastern Europe. Meanwhile, the assertion of Soviet control in Czechoslovakia in 1968-9 gave the Soviet leaders greater confidence in developing relations with the West. President Nixon assured the Soviet Union that the US 'would not seek to exploit Eastern Europe to obtain strategic advantage against the Soviet Union', because the American 'pursuit of negotiation and détente is meant to reduce existing tensions, not to stir up new ones'. From 1970 onwards, the main immediate danger from the West appeared to be that of ideological infection rather than as a result of any Western policy to 'destabilize' Eastern Europe – the rolling back of frontiers was a thing of the past.

What were the reasons for the policies towards the West pursued by the individual states in the years from 1956? Have the motivations and objectives substantially altered in the following years?

Poland

In Poland, there were three main strands in the opening to the West in the early years of Gomulka's leadership. The first aim was to obtain economic benefit through the diversification of trading links and through the import from the West of products which Poland needed for the modernization of its economy. The second aim was to develop a foreign policy which would help to legitimize the regime by providing evidence of Poland's sovereignty and by erasing some of the stigma of the slavish subservience to the Soviet Union which had characterized the Stalinist era. The third aim was to develop a pattern of contacts with the outside world which would take more adequate account of Poland's Western cultural orientation and which would permit broader human and cultural interchange with Western states. These aims lost much of their meaning as the Gomulka regime ossified in the 1960s and reverted to a more isolationist concept of socialism; they were however to reappear in the 1970s under Gierek.

In the early years of Gomulka's power, the balance between these strands was roughly equal. Poland's initial interest in obtaining economic assistance from the West, notably in the form of credits, food and raw materials from the United States, can be seen as a practical response to the austerity of the Stalinist period. Gomulka was well aware that the workers' riots in Poznan in June 1956 were entirely due, and the unrest in Warsaw in October 1956 at least partly due, to the stringent economic policies of his predecessors which had achieved minimal increases in living standards. The first US credit of $94 million was granted in 1957, a year after Gomulka's advent to power, mainly for the purchase of grain. This was followed by a series of further similar credits which, by the end of 1963, had amounted to $537 million.[1] Poland concurrently obtained substantial quantities of Soviet grain, but this was against immediate payment in kind, whereas the payment of US grain was to a frozen zloty account, with generous repayment terms. Although Gomulka reportedly assured Khrushchev that there were no strings attached to the US credits, the Polish move evidently aroused some Soviet suspicions. *Pravda* cautioned in May 1958 that: 'The imperialists do not give anything to anybody for nothing. Everybody knows that American economic aid leads in one form or another to economic and political dependence.'[2] While this warning was directed ostensibly at Yugoslavia, it was assumed at the time that Moscow also had Poland in mind. At least equally important, Poland was accorded MFN treatment by the US in 1957. This was based on the somewhat debatable proposition put forward by the US administration, and swallowed by Congress, that Poland was not a country 'under Soviet domination'. Until 1976, when Romania received MFN treatment from the US, Poland was the only bloc country to be accorded this preferential status.

Trade with the West developed steadily during the 1960s and included imports of capital goods and of technology which were either unobtainable in the East or obtainable only in inferior quality. Poland lacked the ability to achieve any rapid increase in its hard-currency earnings, given the uncompetitive nature of its industry and its limited capacity to increase exports of raw materials, of which coal continued to be the most important. If, however, Western goods could be provided on credit, this offered a solution to the immediate resource dilemma. As the 1960s progressed, the Poles showed a growing interest in obtaining credits from the West. However, the growth of trade with the developed West was less than dramatic. Between 1960 and 1970 it approximately doubled. This compared with a slightly more than doubling of Poland's trade with Comecon countries, with the Soviet Union naturally foremost. Poland's policy of accepting Western credits was of modest proportions and in line with that of the Soviet Union, which took an essentially similar view of the opportunities presented by East–West trade.

The economic policy initiated by the Gierek leadership at the end of 1970 was of a different order. The 'technocrats' who then assumed charge of economic and trade policy turned to the West as a way of making the difficult switch from extensive to intensive economic growth without jeopardy to the living standards of ordinary Poles. They also hoped to be able thereby to avert the need for decentralizing reform of the economy, which would have threatened the party's and bureaucracy's monopoly of power. By means of massive borrowing in the West (at a time of recession in the West when US and European banks were conveniently replete with funds), the government set in hand a huge investment programme designed both to raise living standards at home and to enable Poland to increase its exports, particularly to the West; the aim thereby was to earn the hard currency required to repay the massive borrowings, and the intention was to balance the trade account by 1980. In the first half of the 1970s, the investment spurt was accompanied by large increases in money income (real wages in 1971-5 were claimed by the authorities to have risen by no less than a total of 40 per cent), and many observers, foreign as well as Polish, believed that a Polish economic miracle might be in the making.[3] But in the second half of the 1970s, the outlook fast deteriorated. Poland was unable to achieve the desired level of exports, owing partly to the fact of continuing recession in the West and partly to Polish inexperience in the difficult art of marketing (and providing good service facilities for) their new lines in highly competitive Western economies. Meanwhile, there was a sharp contraction in the growth of real incomes, a series of poor harvests, and failure to meet popular demand for consumer goods (stimulated by the huge wage increases of the early 1970s). By the beginning of 1979, it had become evident that the hoped-for balancing of the trade accounts by 1980 was no longer realistic. Meanwhile Poland's indebtedness increased dramatically from $2.5 billion (net) in 1973 to an estimated $20 billion (gross) at the end of 1979, and an estimated $26 billion (gross) in the spring of 1981. By 1975, Poland's scale of debts and its debt-service ratio was far higher than those of any other East European country. By 1980, over half of Poland's trade was with non-communist countries, though the Soviet Union still accounted for approximately one-third.

Poland's acceptance of US and other Western credits, although (as noted) arousing some Soviet suspicion in Gomulka's early years, had little influence on the direction of Polish foreign policy, which has been closely aligned with Moscow's during the past two decades. President Nixon's stopover in Warsaw in 1959 was in the wake of a visit to Moscow. Poles warmly welcomed the thaw in US–Soviet relations in 1959-60, and later in 1963, but once setbacks to those relations occurred (for instance, after the Cuban missile crisis), Poland quickly followed the Soviet lead. Polish diplomatic moves, such as the launching of the Rapacki Plan in 1958 and the Gomulka Plan of 1963 – although genuine Polish initiatives, in the sense that they were apparently conceived independently by Poles – were aimed primarily at mitigating and containing what was seen jointly in Warsaw and Moscow as the threat from West Germany, and above all at preventing any possibility of the FRG acquiring nuclear weapons. The distinctly Polish element was that, if successful, these initiatives would have created a situation in which the third Polish objective — that of enabling Poland to develop links with the West in harmony with her historical and cultural tradition – would have been assisted.[4] Much the same could be said for the Polish proposal for a European conference on disarmament, launched in 1979. This reflected a genuine Polish national interest in reducing tensions in Eastern Europe, while remaining closely in line with overall post-Helsinki Soviet policies, with their emphasis on the need for 'military détente'.

Poland's relations with the US deteriorated from 1965, in line with the Soviet Union's, because of the intensification of the war in Vietnam. However, this did not prevent relations with de Gaulle's France from blossoming. The Polish Foreign Minister visited Paris in September 1965 and President de Gaulle paid a state visit to Poland in 1966. Poland also developed good relations with the other leading West European countries, including the UK and Italy. The marked increase in official contacts with Western states, and of exchange of high-level visits during the 1970s, was broadly in line with Soviet policy in the era of 'mature détente'. Gierek's enthusiasm for increased contacts with the West also contained a personal element: Gierek's early experience of living in France and Belgium during World War II whetted his appetite for travelling to the West and for developing close contacts with West European leaders, such as Helmut Schmidt and Valéry Giscard d'Estaing.

The main difference between the development of Poland's foreign policy in the early years of Gomulka's leadership, and its later development under Gierek, was that the emphasis shifted from concern about the need to shore up the distinctly 'Polish way' of constructing socialism to a preoccupation with the cultural, and especially the economic, benefits of Western links. In 1956-69, Gomulka saw the development of Western connections as a complement to the assertion of a degree of autonomy in domestic policy. He was determined to ensure that ideology was not interpreted by the Soviet Union in ways which would seriously constrict his internal freedom of manoeuvre: hence the constant Polish insistence during these years that there should be no 'subordinate' or 'superior' parties in the international communist movement. The example of Yugoslav success in buttressing its position *vis-à-vis* the Soviet Union through the establishment of Western links clearly had some influence on Gomulka in these early years. However, at no point did Gomulka show interest in imitating Yugoslavia in developing a foreign policy (as distinct from an internal policy) which differed on fundamental issues from that of the Soviet Union. Indeed, it appeared by 1960 that he was prepared to accept leadership and guidance in the field of foreign policy as the price for maintaining the leeway he had acquired to manage Poland's domestic affairs in a less than (ideologically) orthodox way.[5]

By the second half of the 1960s, Gomulka's interest in continuing the ideological fight against acceptance of the Soviet Union's 'leading role' in the socialist camp was fast evaporating. The relative liberalism of 1956-8 had given way to increasingly repressive policies which led to internal discontent. By 1968, when student disturbances and unrest of intellectuals were seen as a direct challenge to the regime, he had developed into one of the most conformist of the bloc leaders, as evidenced by his warm support for the Soviet intervention in Czechoslovakia in 1968. Although Gierek introduced a new style into the economic management of the country and further developed relations with the West in all spheres, he in no way attempted to challenge the Soviet Union's assumed prerogative of guiding and co-ordinating foreign policy of bloc states. There was no attempt in the 1970s to revive the argument about the ideological basis for Soviet hegemony. The most authoritative statement of the principles underlying the Brezhnev Doctrine was enunciated by Brezhnev in Warsaw in November 1968 during the Fifth Congress of the PUWP. In 1976, Gierek made a particularly effusive acknowledgement of Soviet leadership in the bloc when he declared that: 'Without solidarity with the Communist Party of the Soviet Union it is impossible to strengthen the unity of the states of the socialist system or to strengthen the international unity of the communist and workers' parties, which function in various conditions but struggle for the same fundamental objectives. One's attitude towards the CPSU and to the Soviet Union is the most tested criterion of one's real attitude to the unity of the socialist and anti-imperialist forces.'[6]

The distinctly Polish aspect of Polish foreign policy in the 1970s was the zeal with which the Polish authorities exploited the new leeway they had been offered in developing links with the West, in contrast with the foot-dragging Czechoslovaks and East Germans. Amongst the many positive steps taken during the decade were the improvement of relations with the Vatican, which resulted (in 1971-2) in the transformation of the six Western episcopal areas of Poland into bishoprics; the visit to Poland of President Nixon in 1972, which led to increased US economic support for Poland; the conclusion of a second major agreement with the FRG in 1975 whereby Poland obtained substantial FRG financial help in return for undertaking to allow 125,000 ethnic Germans to emigrate; and Gierek's visit to the Vatican in 1977 followed by the historic visit by the Polish Pope to Poland two years later.

The third objective of bringing Poland's cultural life into keeping with its traditions and with Poland's European heritage was an important element in Gierek's policies, though not Gomulka's, towards the West. Gomulka was anti-intellectual and suspicious of the West. Nevertheless, it was in the early post-1956 period that the foundations were laid for Poland's opening to the West. The cornerstone was the major cultural exchange programme agreed with the US (1958) which provided for 300 Polish scholars and scientists to visit the US annually, under programmes of the Ford and Rockefeller foundations. In the 1960s, the increasingly repressive internal policies of the Gomulka regime were only very partially reflected in the area of travel and cultural contact with the West. Poles were only in fairly rare instances refused permission to travel abroad,[7] and there was an increasing influx of foreign tourists; huge numbers of the *Polonia* community returned to their homeland for family visits. The number of Poles visiting Western countries rose from negligible proportions in the early 1950s to a level of 539,000 in 1978, and 708,000 in 1980. By the mid-1960s, more Western films were already being shown in Poland than Soviet films. In the 1970s these trends accelerated and Poland's 'liberal' image amongst bloc states became more conspicuous: whereas in the mid-1960s, Hungary and Czechoslovakia had been in the lead, Poland had arguably taken the lead by the mid-1970s.

Amongst the influences which reinforced Poland's links with the West was the signature of the Helsinki Final Act. Although arguably this had greater symbolic than practical influence in the countries of Eastern Europe, it was seen by the regime as a confirmation not only of the territorial status quo but also of Poland's place in a Europe which, even if sharply divided on ideological grounds, had a common cultural heritage. The regime's interest in this aspect was also reflected in Gierek's visit to the Vatican in 1977 and, still more importantly, in the visit of the Pope to Poland in 1979. This visit, which was impossible to justify in strictly ideological terms, represented both an acknowledgement by the Polish government of the importance of national traditions, and a confession of its own weakness in mobilizing popular support. If, however, Gierek hoped to boost his own prestige through the papal visit, it was a strategy which clearly failed.

Czechoslovakia

In Czechoslovakia, the opening to the West ran an erratic course. In the last years of the Novotný government, increasing attention was paid to the possibilities of developing links with the West and the advantages these might offer Czechoslovakia, especially in the economic field. This interest stemmed from the evidence of economic failure, about which the CPC showed growing concern (as was first evident at the Twelfth Party Congress in December 1962). Under the Third Five-Year Plan for 1961-5, national income was supposed to rise by 42 per cent, industrial output by 56 per cent and agricultural output by 22 per cent. The actual increases achieved were 10 per cent for national income and 29 per cent for industrial output, while farm output actually dropped by 0.4 per cent. A pilot 'new economic system', reflecting market elements and a higher degree of decentralization, was ready by 1965, but encountered strong opposition from conservatives in the CPC. The ideas in this reform, which were developed by Ota Sik amongst others, owed much to the work of Lange and Brus in Poland, and to a lesser extent, to the Yugoslav experience. Sik and his team of economists attributed some of the blame for the past economic failure to special factors – the disruption (on Soviet instructions) of trade with China, heavy demands placed on Czechoslovak industry to meet Soviet military requirements, the weather, and Khrushchev's policy of forcefully 'catching up and overtaking' the capitalist world. They also believed that the development of trade with the West would help to make Czechoslovak industry more efficient and more competitive. Because of the opposition encountered, the economic reform did not properly get off the ground until after Novotný's fall in January 1968.

The steps taken to reorient Czechoslovakia's trade in the period before January 1968 were four. The most important was the negotiation of a trade agreement with the Federal Republic of Germany, and the agreement that trade missions should be opened in Frankfurt and Prague, in August 1967. The fact that the Novotný regime should have done this shortly after the Soviet Union had made plain its extreme displeasure at the action of the Romanian government in establishing diplomatic relations with the Federal Republic demonstrated how growing interest in economic ties with West Germany had permeated even the still predominantly conservative Czechoslovak leadership.

The 'reform communists', who were in the ascendant from January until the Soviet invasion in August 1968, had as one of their clear aims that of diversifying Czechoslovakia's trade and developing economic links with the West. The motivation for this was largely, though not entirely, economic. The reform leaders believed that the key to improving economic efficiency and boosting economic growth was to open the Czechoslovak market to the pressures of world markets, by diversifying her credit patterns and by removing various surcharges and subsidies from the prices of the foreign market. The basic premise was that the isolation of the Czechoslovak economy had created major distortions of the economy, the effects of which had included stagnation in living standards and a failure of industry to compete in non-Comecon markets. The April 1968 Action Programme stated that the development of economic relations would continue to be based on co-operation with the Soviet Union and other members of Comecon. At the same time, however, it stated that 'we shall also actively support the development of economic relationships with all other countries of the world which show interest in such relations, on the basis of equality, mutual advantage and without discrimination'. The overall objective was described as a 'phased opening of our economy to the world markets', the aim of which would be to create conditions for the convertibility of Czechoslovak currency.[8] The aim of 'opening up' the Czechoslovak economy was closely linked with the belief that the standard of living must be soon raised, and that there should be major shifts from investment in heavy industry, which had so drained Czechoslovak resources, to investment in the production of consumer and agricultural goods, housing, services and other items which would ease the lot of ordinary Czechs and Slovaks. The reformers were fully aware that such changes would take time to produce the desired results.

In the realm of foreign policy, the goals of the reformers were relatively modest. On all possible occasions, they were at pains to stress Czechoslovakia's continuing loyalty to the Warsaw Pact. There were even some doubts as to whether a section on 'foreign policy' needed to be included in the April Action Programme. When it was decided that, after all, a section on international relations was required, every effort was made to demonstrate the reform leaders' intention of maintaining the existing alliances. Emphasis was placed on the need for the fulfilment of Czechoslovakia's 'internationalist' obligations. However, the formulation in the Action Programme relating to the Federal Republic may have been interpreted by the Soviet Union as betokening a possible readiness to follow in the footsteps of Romania (January 1967) in developing links with the Federal Republic, independently of the rest of the Warsaw Pact. The relevant section of the Action Programme (which was significantly one of the few sections reproduced in full in the *Pravda* summary of the Programme) stated that: 'Our geographical position, as well as the need and capacities of an industrial country, require us to carry out a more active European policy aimed at the promotion of mutually advantageous relations with all states and international organizations, and safeguarding collective security of the European continent. We shall consistently proceed from the existence of two German states, from the fact that the German Democratic Republic, as the first socialist state on German territory, is an important peace element in Europe, from the necessity of giving support to the realistic forces in the German Federal Republic, while resisting neo-Nazi and revanchist tendencies. The Czechoslovak people want peace with all nations.'[9] There is in fact no evidence that the Czechoslovak leadership was planning any move towards the FRG which would have been capable of representation as a breaking of ranks in the alliance, Romanian-style. But the Soviet, GDR and Polish leaders appear to have been influenced by the fact of increasing exchange of high-level visitors from Bonn and by the perceptible diminution of anti-FRG propaganda in the Czechoslovak press. The Action Programme also called for a more active Czechoslovak foreign policy, with greater initiative being taken in the United Nations; but this does not appear to have caused anything like the suspicions aroused by contacts with the FRG. The Soviet leadership probably calculated that the Dubček leadership would be strongly tempted to follow Romania in accepting large credits from Bonn as a way of rehabilitating the economy, and that this risked impairing bloc solidarity. Czechoslovakia's central geographical and strategic position, and her propinquity to the GDR, with whom she also shared a similar state of economic development, made the threat to bloc solidarity almost certainly more serious in Soviet eyes than that represented by Romania. The Soviet leaders may well have also had wider misgivings about the European thrust of the reform movement, given the evident desire of the reform communists to re-establish Czechoslovakia as a member of the European family of nations both culturally and politically, albeit within the Eastern alliance system.

The precise extent to which the Soviet Union's perception of Prague's foreign policy and external trade policy influenced the eventual decision to invade is a question which cannot be answered with any certitude. The Soviet leaders appear to have been concerned above all about the risk that the leading role of the Czechoslovak Communist Party would be subverted, and that a non-socialist form of government, or one in which non-socialist elements had a strong influence, would emerge from the debris. It seems in fact likely that the internal and external dangers presented by Dubček's policies and by spontaneous forces in Czecho-slovakia were closely linked in the Soviet assessment: a breakdown of internal controls would inevitably lead to unreliability in external policies. Soviet fears on this score were undoubtedly reinforced by such episodes as the press conference given by General Prchlik, in which he openly criticized the way in which the Soviet Union treated its partners in the Warsaw Pact.[10] The public airing of anti-Soviet prejudices threatened to create a dangerously anti-Soviet public atmosphere which a weak communist leadership would be unable to control.

There is no evidence that the Soviet Union expressed opposition to the Czechoslovak reformers' plan for economic reform. The Czechoslovak interest in opening the Czech economy to the 'pressures of world markets' was not in itself a matter for serious Soviet concern; this was similar to the objectives of others in Eastern Europe interested in eco-nomic reform, and was to a certain extent reflected in the Hungarian New Economic Mechanism, also launched in 1968. Soviet economists in the mid-1960s were themselves interested in similar reform ideas.[11] However, issues of economic reform and reform of the political system became so closely intertwined in the public debate during the Prague spring and summer that it was natural for the Husák leadership which succeeded Dubček to react to each with equal vigour: the economic reforms were dismantled as ruthlessly as the political. Ironically, the international aspect of the reform programme which caused the Soviet Union most anxiety —the fear that West Germany would seek to prise Czechoslovakia away from the socialist alliance — was shortly to evaporate. Once the Soviet Union had normalized its own relations with the FRG in 1970 and the way was clear for other East European states to follow suit, the new Czechoslovak leadership found itself in the curious position of being urged by the Soviet Union to proceed quickly to the normalization of Czechoslovak-FRG relations. The Husák government embarked on this course reluctantly, after much Soviet prodding, and the negotiations with the FRG were characterized by considerable Czech heel-dragging up to the final agreement reached in 1974.

The Husák regime has closely controlled contact with the West in the evident belief that this assists its internal plans. Normalization has been achieved at the cost of insulating Czechoslovakia from the capitalist world. This policy is reflected in all fields. Czechoslovak trade with the West has been maintained at a level which, although increasing in volume, has stayed at a fairly constant percentage of total trade. In 1965, Czechoslovakia did 26.8 per cent of its trade with non-socialist countries. In 1978, the figure was 27.3 per cent. Tourism has followed a similar pattern. 406,000 Czechs and Slovaks visited capitalist countries in 1979 as against one million from these countries who visited Czechoslovakia.[12] Ordinary Czechoslovaks found it difficult to obtain exit visas and those who were known for their critical views towards the regime frequently found that their only option, if they wished to travel to the West, was to go into 'permanent emigration'.

The regime's restrictive policies also found expression in frosty relations with the Vatican. In early 1980, ten out of thirteen resident bishoprics in Czechoslovakia were without resident bishops. An acute shortage of religious literature was noted, and priests were frequently detained or otherwise harassed. The government was firm in preventing any increase in the small number of priests who were being trained or in those who were performing actual duties.

The most publicized aspect of the government's repressive policy was its treatment of signatories to Charter 77, a document aimed at drawing public attention to the discrepancy between Czechoslovakia's international commitments and the Husák regime's domestic practices in the field of human rights. The internal significance of this is examined in Chapter 6. Externally, the persecution of Charterists has harmed the government's image and has caused embarrassment to other Warsaw Pact countries, for instance when a major trial of Charterists was announced just as the main 1977 CSCE review-meeting was getting under way in Belgrade. It is not known whether the Soviet Union was consulted about the timing of this trial, although it seems probable that the Russians gave general approval to Czechoslovak policy towards dissenters.

Romania

The external policy pursued by the Romanian leadership has shown remarkable consistency in its general thrust since the early 1960s. This has been combined with considerable tactical flexibility. The two major motives of Gheorghiu-Dej and Ceauşescu appear to have been to enhance the authority of their leadership by closely identifying themselves with patently Romanian national goals, and to promote a Romanian policy of national economic development which has at times diverged from Soviet policies for the bloc as a whole. Economic links with the West and with the Third World have served both these goals. They have helped to provide a counterweight to the Soviet Union and have brought direct economic benefits to Romania. The history of Romania's foreign policy has been well covered in academic literature[13] and it would be otiose to repeat the details here. But certain salient facts are worth recapitulating. As noted, the events of 1956 probably did much to convince the Romanian leadership that it was not sufficient to look to the Soviet Union to guarantee survival. While the Soviet Union would not allow a Warsaw Pact state to be subverted by capitalism, it had shown in Hungary that it was not prepared to back leaders of a bloc state such as Rákosi who had plainly forfeited popular confidence. The issue which served as a catalyst for Romania's assertion of independence was Khrushchev's attempt to introduce supranational planning into Comecon. The principles of the international socialist division of labour as conceived by Khrushchev threatened to make Romania's under-development permanent. By turning to the West, Romania might enjoy the prospect of substantial economic growth in the short term without having to undergo the long-term disadvantage of enforced autarky within the bloc. This at any rate was how Gheorghiu-Dej and Ceauşescu came to respond to the Soviet Union's lack of enthusiasm for rapid Romanian industrialization, and its attempts to achieve the international socialist division of labour along the lines which would have favoured the growth of industry in the already developed countries at the expense of the least developed.

The first stirrings of an autonomous foreign policy came in the early 1960s when Gheorghiu-Dej complemented his opposition to Khrushchev's supranational plans by attempting to mediate in the ripening Sino-Soviet dispute. The latter conflict presented Romania with valuable scope for asserting her interests at this time. Until 1965, China was still regarded by the USSR as a member of the socialist family. Khrushchev's ouster in 1964 was partly linked with growing criticism within the CPSU of his clumsy handling of relations with China, and the incoming Brezhnev leadership was keenly interested in repairing the damage. The Romanian attempts at mediation ended in failure. The Romanians, in order to defend their position and to register the significance of their diplomatic foray, in April 1964 issued the Romanian 'Declaration of Independence'. This argued that their policies were of a principled nature, based on such internationally accepted concepts as national sovereignty and equality of states. The Declaration was immediately followed by the dispatch of Gaston Marin, the Romanian Minister of Foreign Trade, to Washington in June, where he secured a promise of increased US economic activity and technological assistance (albeit on a very modest scale). A month later, the Foreign Minister, Maurer, visited Paris where the French and Romanian governments agreed to increase both economic and cultural co-operation. This was translated into a form of agreement in February 1965.The Franco–Romanian agreement coincided with the signature of a new trade protocol with the Soviet Union covering the years 1966-70. These events were the first steps in a Romanian balancing act which gained complexity as the years passed.

Some writers have characterized Romania's policy as one of periodic redefinition of the boundaries of autonomy. Another way of describing it is as a series of moves to test the limits of Soviet tolerance in the area of foreign policy and its control of bloc affairs. Amongst the weapons employed in this game have been development of Romanian links outside the Warsaw Pact, especially with the developed West, with China and Yugoslavia and, later, with the non-aligned states. Developments of particular note in the assertion of autonomy have been Romania's establishment of diplomatic relations with the FRG in January 1967; her refusal to sever diplomatic relations with Israel in the wake of the Arab-Israeli war of 1967; Ceauşescu's condemnation of the Soviet invasion of Czechoslovakia in 1968 and his formation of a people's militia, purportedly to defend the homeland; the visits to Romania of President de Gaulle (in 1968) and Nixon (in 1969); Romania's refusal to endorse a Soviet proposal for the condemnation of China –following the Ussuri frontier incidents – at the Warsaw Pact PCC meeting in December 1969; Ceauşescu's visit to Peking in 1971; Romania's entry to the IMF and the IBRD in 1972; her admittance to the Group of 77 in 1976; the visit of Ceauşescu to Peking in May 1978 and the return visit of Hua Guofeng to Romania in August of the same year; Romania's refusal to give public endorsement to a number of Soviet foreign policy aims, including its policies in respect of Israel and of Vietnam in its war against China, again at the Warsaw Pact Summit of November 1978; Romanian unilateral announcements of plans to reduce military spending in 1978 and in 1980, in apparent contradiction to Pact goals; and Romanian gestures of dissatisfaction with the Soviet intervention in Afghanistan, such as their non-participation in the United Nations General Assembly vote on a condemnatory resolution in January 1980.

In practical terms, the opening to the West has brought Romania two main advantages. In the economic sphere the growth of trade and economic links, although fairly modest in the 1960s, assumed impressive

47

proportions in the 1970s. The proportion of Romania's trade with non-Comecon countries increased from 26.7 per cent in 1963 to 52.2 per cent in 1977. Particularly important was the increase in trade with the United States, the FRG, France and Canada. In the 1970s Romania signed a number of industrial co-operation and joint-venture agreements with Western firms,[14] such as the agreement with Data Products Ltd of the United States and the £300 million contract for the construction of BAC 1-11 aircraft in Romania (1978). Romania obtained substantial loans from the IMF and the IBRD; the latter had extended loans totalling approximately $450 million by 1979. Romania was granted substantial credits by a number of Western countries during the 1970s, including Canada, the FRG and Italy. A major deal for the purchase of Canadian CANDIA nuclear reactors, as the basis for the Romanian nuclear programme, was concluded in 1978. Romania obtained MFN status from the United States in 1975. Trade with the US is being developed rapidly, as well as with Western Europe, and Romania is the only East European country to have trade promotion offices in the US (a total of five). In 1980, an agreement was signed with the EEC allowing preferential access for ninety-four Romanian products.

The development of economic links with China has been less important though politically significant. In 1971, imports from China were about two-thirds of those from the FRG (one and a half times those from the US); in 1976 the proportion was one-half of the FRG and two-thirds of the US share. Items which have been imported by Romania have included machine tools, equipment for the metallurgical industry and factories and plants for the chemical industry. There have also been reports of the delivery of small quantities of oil in 1979/80. Romania has developed close economic links with Yugoslavia. These have encompassed major joint projects for the construction of large hydroelectric stations on the Danube and the joint development of a fighter aircraft. Also of some interest has been the development of links with Third-World countries. The percentage of trade with these countries has risen from 7.3 per cent in 1965 to approximately 20 per cent in 1979. Romanian interest in obtaining new sources of raw materials was the main reason for the major tour by Ceausescu of black African and North African states in early 1979, though few practical results have yet materialized.

Economic links with non-communist states have been politically significant in serving to decrease the degree of Romanian dependence on the Soviet Union. At the same time the exchange of high-level visits with non-communist countries has helped to boost Romania's image of autonomy. The friendship of a variety of states outside the Warsaw Pact has also offered Romania a certain reassurance in the pursuit of that policy in the event of a major dispute with the Soviet Union. This reassurance has never been put to the test, but it is noteworthy that the United States has, on at least two occasions, offered support when Romania has been under Soviet pressure. At the end of August 1968, after the Soviet Union had sharply criticized Romania as well as Yugoslavia for opposition to its intervention in Czechoslovakia, and when the US press carried rumours of Soviet manoeuvres near Romania's borders, Washington let it be known that it would 'view with the utmost seriousness' any Soviet intervention in Yugoslavia or Romania. This robust statement contrasted curiously with the entirely passive approach of the US administration in the run-up to the invasion of Czechoslovakia. A later demonstration of US support came in 1979 when President Carter sent the Treasury Secretary, Michael Blumenthal, to Romania as his special envoy to 'reaffirm to the Romanian people and to President Ceauşescu the importance we attach to Romania's independence and to US-Romanian friendship'. This was at a time of particular Romanian–Soviet tension, following the exchange of presidential visits with China and the disruptive stance adopted by Romania at the Warsaw Pact Summit in November 1978. For their part, the Chinese have demonstrated support for Romania and in 1971 went so far as to speak of the two countries being 'comrades in arms' in the defence of independence. However, it should be borne in mind that neither country has made, nor seems likely to make, any commitment to offer support of more than a diplomatic kind. Whereas the US and other Western states have adopted a clear deterrent posture in respect of Yugoslavia, which must reduce any possibility of the application of the Brezhnev Doctrine to that country, this is not the US posture in respect of Romania. For China there are obvious logistical as well as other reasons which would rule out the provision of effective military support, barring any decision to launch all-out war against the Soviet Union.

Romania placed considerable hopes in the CSCE as a vehicle for further extending its scope for autonomy in foreign relations and for promoting its concept of a Europe based on mutual respect for national sovereignty rather than a continent based on confrontation of military blocs. They were to some extent successful in securing the incorporation into the Helsinki Final Act of a number of the concepts dear to them which included the principle of non-intervention in internal affairs. However, the follow-up to Helsinki has nowhere near lived up to the promise the Romanians saw in it. Although at Belgrade the Romanians tried, partly in informal alliance with non-aligned and neutral states, to obtain a constructive outcome which would give new impetus to the principles of Helsinki, the outcome was almost entirely negative. The meeting served to demonstrate the limitations of the effectiveness of Romanian actions in East-West negotiations, where the Soviet Union adopts a contrary position and is prepared to throw its full weight behind it.

The three most serious challenges to the Soviet Union have occurred either at times when the USSR has been actively promoting a policy of détente (in 1971 and 1978) or when (in August-September 1968) it was anxious to prevent its military action in Czechoslovakia from jeopardizing the chances of improved relations with Western Europe and the US. On each occasion, the Romanian government drew back in the face of Soviet pressure: in 1968 the provocative condemnation of the invasion of Czechoslovakia was followed by a moderation of criticism of Soviet policy, and in 1970 a new bilateral Romanian-Soviet treaty was signed with the Russians;[15] in 1971 a Soviet campaign of pressure against Romania at the time of Ceauşescu's visit to Peking resulted in a halting of Romania's attempt to forge a special relationship with China; in August 1978, the Romanians were careful to reduce to a minimum the provocative aspects of the visit of Hua Guofeng to Bucharest (most notably in avoiding open criticism of the Soviet Union—though Hua could not be deterred from referring to 'hegemonism'). Again, the Soviet Union and other Warsaw Pact countries waged a press campaign, accusing the Chinese of attempting to drive a wedge between Romania and its Pact allies, but on this occasion Soviet displeasure appears to have been less acute than in 1971. The Romanians were not deterred from registering (at the Warsaw Pact Summit in November 1978) their opposition to increased Pact defence expenditure and opposing Soviet attempts to obtain WTO backing for its anti-Chinese and Middle Eastern policies.

The tone of Romanian pronouncements on such sensitive issues has however moderated since the clear setback for détente resulting from the Soviet invasion of Afghanistan at the end of 1979. The Romanians' refusal to endorse the Soviet action, while significant, was done without undue provocation.[16] Romania helped to assuage Soviet sensitivities by extending its criticism to *all* those interfering in Afghan affairs, which in the Romanian view also included Pakistan. When Prime Minister Verdet visited Peking at the end of 1980, he made a point of stopping off in Moscow both on the way there and on the return journey.

The evidence does not demonstrate any precise correlation between the health of détente and the vigour of Romanian 'autonomy'. But there seems little doubt, as the events of 1980/81 seemed to demonstrate, that there is at least some connection. It is also clear that a major setback to the CSCE process would frustrate Romanian ambitions to assert the interests of 'small and medium-sized states'.

There are two other aspects of Romanian foreign policy which deserve a mention. First, Romanian opposition to Soviet proposals in the WTO and Comecon fora may be welcome to others in the socialist family who have similar attitudes but would prefer not to have to express them openly: Romania serves in this respect as a stalking horse. Second,

Romania's special links outside the family, such as those with the Group of 77 and with China, may on occasion prove useful to the Soviet Union itself. Soviet interest in this aspect may have accounted for the fact that Prime Minister Verdet stopped off twice in Moscow when visiting China in late 1980 (as noted above).

A number of commentators on the failure of the Czechoslovak 1968 reform experiment have suggested that Dubček would have had a somewhat better chance of averting Soviet intervention had he been able to develop a network of foreign links on the lines of those developed by Gheorghiu-Dej and Ceauşescu. This is possibly so. However, Romania's success in asserting autonomy has relied heavily on a number of factors which were not present in Czechoslovakia in 1968. Particularly important was the fact that Soviet planners evidently attached much less strategic importance to Romania and Bulgaria than to the three northern tier countries.[17] Almost equally important was the fact that the Romanian leadership was entirely committed to maintaining the communist party's monopoly of power, albeit with one or two unorthodox twists.[18] At the same time, the tight grip in which Ceausescu held the Romanian Communist Party, and the elimination of potential opponents, made any external attempt to secure a change at the top the more potentially hazardous. Finally, the Romanian leaders' professed readiness to defend Romanian territory by military means in the event of intervention doubtless had some influence.

The question is sometimes posed whether Romania's pursuit of autonomy amounts to much more than a device to legitimize the rule of the communist party, and Ceauşescu's own ascendancy, by the proclamation of national slogans. As noted, it can be claimed that Romania has obtained economic benefit from its links with the West. However, as discussed in Chapter 5, this whole policy came under review in the course of 1980-81, and Romanian leaders are now seeking to shift the pattern of their trade eastwards. Apart from trade and credits, rather few tangible benefits have accrued to Romania, although it can be argued that the population has derived advantage from the low level of the government's expenditure on defence (no more than an estimated 1.7 per cent in 1979). As against this, the advantages of the assertion of autonomy in domestic terms should certainly not be minimized. When for example Ceauşescu defied the Soviet Union in 1968 and decreed the creation of a people's militia in the wake of the invasion of Czechoslovakia, this undoubtedly gained him popular support. Subsequent less dramatic anti-Soviet gestures have augmented this and have helped to assuage popular dissatisfaction with the very low growth in living standards. It may indeed well be that the Soviet Union's tolerance of Romanian waywardness is influenced by an understanding of the domestic basis on which 'autonomy' rests.

The significance of CSCE

It is generally assumed that the CSCE process has given some impetus to the trends towards greater contacts, humanitarian and other, and to the freer exchange of information between the two halves of Europe. But it is very difficult to quantify this: many of the improvements that have taken place might well have happened without the signature of the Final Act, and in some cases (especially in the case of Czechoslovakia) it is obvious that policy regarding travel has related at least as much to regimes' internal preoccupations, including their perceptions of their vulnerability to external political influence, as to their CSCE undertakings. Probably the Basket III areas where the best achievements have been registered which can be plausibly linked with a desire to fulfil specific Final Act commitments are those relating to visa-issuing procedures and personal/family reunification/marriage cases. A number of improvements in visa-issuing procedures, on the basis of reciprocal arrangements, have been achieved between the UK and various East European states. The reduction in outstanding family reunification and marriage cases between the UK and the three bloc states surveyed may also reflect a close CSCE connection. In the run-up to Madrid, significant improvements in this area were noted in respect of both Romania and Czechoslovakia. Poland had a good record of implementation in virtually all areas of Basket III of the Final Act. Particularly commendable were the facilities granted foreign journalists during the Pope's visit to Poland in 1979. In this respect, Poland's record contrasted sharply with that of Czechoslovakia, where the activities of Western journalists were severely restricted, and Romania, where in 1980 there were cases of excessive police surveillance of British journalists.

The extent to which the Soviet Union has an interest in the implementation of Basket III provisions is very much open to debate. What is less debatable is that the governments of the more 'liberal' East European states, notably Hungary and Poland, have taken a positive interest in the implementation of many of these provisions, and have been somewhat less averse than the Soviet Union to the idea that follow-up CSCE meetings should take new steps –by agreeing 'new proposals'– to secure better implementation of the provisions of the Final Act in such relatively sensitive areas as human contacts. However, given the hard stance adopted by the Soviet Union at Belgrade, there was in practice little hope of making progress. At Madrid the prospects have looked no better.

East European governments have shown the greatest interest in the disarmament/arms control provisions of Basket I of the Final Act, and in the Basket II (economic) chapter. Interest in the disarmament aspect, reflected in the Polish proposal for a European conference on disarmament which was submitted to the Madrid meeting, is an expression of

Soviet as well as of East European desiderata. The past Polish interest in reducing military tension in central Europe as a path to achieving political goals has already been discussed. There is also a wider East European interest in reducing the risks of East-West military confrontation into which most of the East European states would inevitably be drawn, and in reducing the burden of military expenditure. Interest in Basket II reflects a general appreciation of the benefits of commercial links with the West which long preceded CSCE. Improvements which can be clearly identified with the CSCE follow-up process are not numerous. However, in Czechoslovakia there has been an improvement in the access which Western businessmen have had to end users, and a new law of July 1980 allowed some enterprises to negotiate direct with foreign firms in the conduct of certain forms of trade. In Poland there were indications in 1980-81 that the authorities might be more forthcoming in providing economic statistics of improved quality and quantity, but this appeared to derive more from the country's economic troubles and the consequent need to reassure Western bankers than from a desire to fulfil Final Act provisions.

The development of contacts with the European Community

The attitude of most East European states towards the nascent European Community has been ambivalent. In the early years, East European states adopted a negative posture in accordance with the (1962) Soviet '32 propositions on imperialist integration in Europe', the clear message of which was that the existence of the EEC did not imply the need for co-operation between economic or other blocs. In the 1970s, after Brezhnev had declared himself (1972) in favour of recognizing 'realities' in Europe, the East European posture softened, although there was still no formal official recognition of the Community. Following a first approach by Comecon to the EEC in July 1973, talks between the two bodies have progressed intermittently but fruitlessly since 1975. The possibility of achieving any agreement has been frustrated by a difference of view on the fundamental issue of the respective natures of the two bodies. Whereas Comecon has striven for acknowledgement of equality between them, the Community has taken the (understandable) view that there is no equivalence between the two bodies, since the nature of the integration which has taken place within the Community is very different from that applying amongst the Comecon members. The fact that Community recognition of Comecon as an aqual could also imply acknowledgement of Soviet pre-eminence within that organization has not, it would appear, been lost on East as well as West Europeans.

The Comecon—EEC impasse has not prevented the development of other links in the 1970s between the Community and East European states. The first major landmark was the signature of an agreement on textiles (in 1976) with Romania. Romania also joined the EEC generalized preferences system. The 1976 agreement was followed by the more far-ranging 1980 agreement on industrial products, which interestingly also provided for the regular convocation of joint commissions to discuss issues of economic co-operation. Poland has also developed increasing contacts with the Community, and in 1981 approached it with a request for food aid. (The scale of the Community response is described in Chapter 5.)

In sum, Romania has taken substantial steps in developing contacts with the Community and can expect to derive real benefit. This has, however, been balanced by a continuing refusal—for example, in CSCE negotiations—to accept the Community as purporting to be a *political* bloc. The recent growth in Polish contacts with the Community has been closely linked with its economic troubles. For Czechoslovakia, the Community as such has so far not loomed large.

The benefits

Eastern Europe's opening to the West has brought some political costs as well as benefits, particularly in the period following the signature of the Final Act; these are the subject of Chapter 6. The benefits, viewed from the perspective of the regimes, lie mainly in the economic sphere. For Romania, trade and economic co-operation with the West (and to a lesser extent with the Third World) have brought indisputable advantages and have been one of the essential ingredients in the pursuit of a highly ambitious policy of rapid industrialization. In Poland, growing enthusiasm for trade with the West was replaced by a certain sense of disillusion as the country went into a deep economic crisis in 1979-80. However, as described in Chapter 5, the causes of the crisis owed far more to simple mismanagement than to the westwards orientation of Poland's commerce. Overall, there can be little doubt that trade with the West has made an important contribution to Poland's industrial development. For Czechoslovakia, trade with the West was also useful as a means of obtaining industrial equipment of types unavailable, or only available in inferior quality, in the East.

In the realm of cultural and human contacts, it is arguable that greater benefits from the growing level of East-West interchange have accrued to non-communists in Eastern Europe than to the regimes themselves. Cultural and scientific exchanges, which have been carefully controlled by the authorities, have mostly served the interests both of the regimes and of those in the populations who do not share their values. The same applies to other types of officially sponsored exchanges. The growth of tourism and personal contacts, both of East Europeans travelling to the West and of traffic in the other direction, has been welcome to most

East Europeans for obvious reasons, but has been a source of anxiety to some of the regimes who have feared, in varying degrees, that one result may be to encourage anti-socialist forces and to increase the possibilities for subversion both psychological and physical. The Czechoslovak regime has appeared much preoccupied by these aspects, as has to a lesser extent the Romanian. Similar worries have been aroused by the (mostly rather slight) increases in the exchange of information, though these have been far more marked in Czechoslovakia — where non-communist foreign newspapers are virtually non-existent — than in Poland where by 1980 they could be found in any public reading-room.

In the realm of foreign policy, the opening to the West has had only very limited effects. As seen, Western political interest in Romania may have been of some assistance in the assertion of autonomy. But Romania's relative successes in this field have owed more to other factors. Poland, for a variety of reasons, has not attempted to develop a comparably independent foreign policy. Successive regimes attached priority to safeguarding their room for internal freedom of manoeuvre and were prepared to pay some price for this in their relations with the USSR. The main Polish practical aim has appeared to be to try to exploit points where Soviet and Polish interests more or less coalesced, for instance with the Rapacki Plan. The fact that such attempts have ended in failure was in large part due to circumstances beyond Polish control. At the other end of the spectrum, Czechoslovakia has in recent years, along with the GDR, on a number of occasions adopted positions which were more hardline than that of the Soviet leadership itself. The fleeting experience of reform in 1968 was directed far more to internal than to any external goals: it was the fear of disorder and loss of control, with all of their consequences, rather than the reformers' interest in links with the West, which provoked the decisive Soviet action.

5 The economic outlook

The aim of this chapter is to assess the implications, for the East European states covered, of the pulls of Comecon economic integration on the one hand and the attraction of trade with the West on the other. It first surveys the main changes that have taken place in the 1970s, and looks at the outlook for the 1980s. The attempt is then made to answer what would seem to be the key questions of political importance, particularly the influence of economic dependence on the West on the internal and foreign policies of the East European states.

Poland

The lessons to be drawn from the Polish example are far from straightforward. On a simple reading of events, it might appear that the decision by the Gierek government at the opening of the 1970s to turn to the West for the achievement of rapid economic growth was responsible for the crisis of 1980: the huge foreign credit-financed investment programme of 1971-8, coupled with the payment of large wage increases, produced inflationary tendencies and an overheating of the economy. Yet the Gierek strategy failed to achieve the revitalization and modernization of industry on a scale sufficient to obtain increases in exports, in the second half of the 1970s, which would restore the balance of trade and allow the servicing and repayment of Poland's by then massive foreign debts. While the 1980/81 crisis was by no means concerned only with economic issues, the government's economic failures were the single most important cause of the collapse of its credibility. By 1980 it was obvious to most Poles that a vast chasm had opened up between the claims of the government's propaganda and the actual situation of the country.

Polish criticism of the economic failure made during the summer and autumn of 1980 did not blame the original policy, enunciated shortly after Gierek's election to the First-Secretaryship, of seeking large-scale inflows of capital and technology from the West. However, what has come in for criticism has been the manner in which the policy was implemented, particularly after 1972 when the problems first began to become apparent, and the failure of the planners to maintain adequate control. The 'seven sins' leading to the 1980 crisis were succinctly summarized by Professor Mieczyslaw Mieszczankowski[1] as:

excessive —at times misplaced—investments
excessive indebtedness
excessive growth in incomes
inappropriate agricultural and retail policies
erroneous social policies
atrophy of central planning.

The most fundamental explanation of what went wrong is that the planners and managers of the day were afflicted by excessive optimism and that, having pinned their faith to a policy of import-led growth, they chose to ignore the evidence of impending trouble. The problems were part externally and part internally generated. The Western recession which began in 1973 and reached its peak in the mid-1970s made it more difficult for Poland to export manufactured products for hard currency, and hence to earn enough hard currency to service and repay her mounting debts to foreign banks and other creditors. At the same time, Poland found herself confronted with increasing bills for imported raw materials, particularly oil. Although in the first half of the 1970s Poland was protected by the five-year fixed price she was paying for Soviet oil which accounted for almost all her total oil imports, the shift to a five-year moving average after 1975 caused a worsening of Poland's terms of trade. While she was able to obtain higher prices for exports of Polish coal, this only partially offset the hardship resulting from higher oil prices. The Poles were also confronted, as a result of inflation in the West, with higher prices for imported industrial goods and other Western products. Meanwhile, also mainly as a result of inflation in the West and increasing competition towards the end of the 1970s for bank finance, Poland was compelled to accept new credits (used increasingly to service the growing debt, which by 1976 had reached $11 billion) at higher rates of interest.

Poles have on occasion complained about the allegedly irresponsible behaviour of foreign banks in pressing loans at a time of recession when they were replete with funds. However, no authoritative source has tried to depict this as a major reason for the crisis at the end of the 1970s: the decision whether or not to accept loans and credits was of course entirely in the hands of the Polish central authorities. A slightly more serious criticism is that Western firms, in their enthusiasm to promote business in Poland, resorted to bribery in selling their wares.[2] In this case too, however, it was clear that blame was at least as much apportionable to the Polish alleged recipients, whose dedication to 'socialist values' should have acted as a shield to temptation.

In his persuasive post-mortem on the origins of the crisis, Professor Mieszczankowski suggested that the authorities' fatal mistake was to ignore advice in 1972 to avoid any further acceleration in the rate of growth of the economy, in the light of depletion of the internal reserves of the economy and the signs of impending recession in the West. Instead, the rate of accumulation, which had already risen sharply by 1972, was increased still further after that year, reaching a net figure of 37.8 per cent in 1975 (compared with 27.9 per cent in 1970). Wages continued to grow at an annual claimed rate of approximately 10 per cent. Much of the imported industrial equipment could not be put to immediate use and there were many delays, for instance as a result of inadequate transport facilities for new factories. Meanwhile, production of consumer goods, which was given distinctly lower priority than production of capital goods, failed to keep pace with the large increases in earnings: it is estimated that between 1972 and 1977 wages grew 40 per cent faster than the increase in the production of consumer goods.[3] While the government resorted to increasing imports of consumer goods in addition to producer foods from the West, the whole of the second half of the 1970s was characterized by a marked excess of demand over supply of basic consumer commodities.

The weakness of the agricultural sector was another main cause of the economic malaise. The poor performance of Polish agriculture is not directly related to foreign influences, and it is beyond the scope of this study to analyse its full causes. What was of major importance for Poland's economy and the balance of its trade in the 1970s, however, was the stagnation of grain production, beginning in 1974, and continuing until the end of the decade. This was caused partly by bad weather, but also by a lack of adequate investment in agriculture and by insufficient supply of fertilizers. The problem was compounded by the state policy of giving preference to large state animal-breeding farms, which were extravagant in their consumption of corn (at any rate in the initial phase) at the expense of smallholders who, it was widely thought, could have supplied the market more efficiently. High imports of corn were one of the main reasons for the failure to balance the trade account and for the government's need to resort to further heavy borrowing in the West. In 1978 the amount imported was no less than eight million tons of grain. The import of grain in the early period (1971-4) was accompanied by a growth of animal stock, but in 1974-7, when there was a further rise in grain imports, the stock declined.

The failures in social policy and price policy in the 1970s were closely connected. Short of introducing food rationing, the only way of reconciling the effects of world inflation, the relative scarcity of basic goods, and the escalating earning power of Polish workers was to introduce a more realistic level of prices, particularly for items such as meat which were in short supply. From a strictly economic point of view; the increases announced in December 1970, June 1976 and July 1980 were entirely justifiable, while the government decisions in 1970 and 1976 to rescind the increases were retrograde steps. But as is now well documented, the government was unable, on any of these three occasions, to win the understanding and confidence of the Polish workers. The latter were convinced only of the fact that their living standards were being eroded as a result of policy decisions in which they played no part.

One effect of the Polish planners' commitment to a strategy of accelerating import-led growth was to diminish the possibility of successful economic reform. An attempt at a partial economic reform in 1968-70 had already been undermined as a result of the government's rescinding of more realistically based prices following the workers' riots in 1970. In 1972-3, a new attempt to introduce decentralizing reforms was launched. However, the objective conditions could hardly have been worse: instead of exhibiting the slack which is accepted as highly desirable if not an absolute prerequisite for the successful implementation of a major economic reform, the economy was becoming increasingly taut. In 1975 there was a shift to recentralization, with WOG (large industrial groupings) being deprived of some important elements of their autonomy. Little more was heard of economic reform from the government during the second half of the 1970s. The explanation for the failure of this attempt at reform was no doubt partly connected with the innate conservatism of the Polish bureaucracy, which throughout the post-war period has never shown any enthusiasm for innovation. However, the main explanation would seem to lie in the fact that, just at the moment when the attempt was made, Poland was confronted by growing economic adversities, including a sharp up-turn in consumer demand with consequent heavy pressures on prices and a deteriorating outlook for foreign trade. The instinct of the bureaucracy, in such circumstances, is to grasp the reins of control as tightly as possible in order to limit the damage.

At the opening of the 1980s, Poland was confronted with a similar dilemma to that faced in the mid-1970s, although the situation was more acute. In response to the economic and political crisis of 1980, and under heavy pressure from Solidarity, the new Polish leadership committed itself to a course of economic reform. The commitment was a belated recognition of the view held by many intellectuals and economists, both inside and outside the communist party, that the old economic system had been proved bankrupt, and that thoroughgoing changes were required. The main difference from earlier calls for reform was that in 1980 reform was seen as not simply a desirable means of improving economic performance but, more importantly, as a prerequisite for winning wide public backing for the government's economic policies. At the same time, the economic constraints militating against a smooth process of reform were much more considerable than the (already substantial) constraints encountered in the 1960s and 1970s.

Unsatisfied demand and pressure on prices were still more serious problems at the end of 1980 than in the mid-1970s. The size of Poland's debt (estimated at over $26 billion gross in April 1981) was certain to limit Poland's freedom of economic manoeuvre for many years to come. The debt-service ratio seems likely, as of 1981, to exceed 100 per cent. Although Poland was able before and during the 1980 crisis to obtain substantial new loans and credits from Western banks and governments, as well as assistance from the USSR and her Comecon partners,[4] it was obvious that it would become increasingly difficult to raise new money to help Poland service and repay her debts. Poland's balance of payments performance proved significantly worse than planned in both 1979 and 1980, and increased interest rates in the West have added approximately $1 billion to the annual service charge, which is likely to come to $2.5–3 billion in the coming years.[5] The Finance Minister gave a clear warning of future stringency when he noted in October 1980 that 'we will have to live with our debt for many years, relatively decreasing its weight'. The condition for the latter hope would be the adoption of 'tough' measures, including the fixing of prices to reflect value, of wages to reflect actual production, and the making of investments only when it could be established with certainty that they would pay off.

In the 1980s, the government's scope for achieving substantially increased exports will depend on many factors, including the success of the plans for economic reform. Assuming that the new economic measures include new incentives for managers and workers in producing for export, this could provide a welcome (though only gradually felt and at present hardly quantifiable) boost. In the short term, however, the authorities have little latitude. Substantial increases in exports of raw materials can be achieved only if internal consumption is curtailed.

On the other side of the ledger, there will be a growing requirement for oil imports. In 1981-5, Poland's supplies of oil from the Soviet

Union will be stabilized at the 1980 level, and it will be necessary to import as much as 6-7 million tons per annum from the non-communist world by 1985 (against 2.5 million from this source in 1978). Poland will also import substantially increased quantities of natural gas from the Soviet Union, but part of this will represent Soviet payment for the Polish contribution to the Orenburg gas pipeline.

It is clear that Poland will not be able to rely on the energy sector for achieving a substantial improvement in the balance of trade: in hard-currency trade, the rise in oil imports from outside the Soviet Union will more than offset gains from exports of Polish coal and other raw materials. As in the 1970s, Poland will have to look primarily to its manufacturing industry to achieve the bulk of the hoped-for increases in export earnings. If, as was forecast by the IMF in 1980, the main developed Western countries move out of recession in the second half of 1981, this should give a fillip to Poland's exports of manufactured goods. Poland may also expect to increase further its trade with developing countries, partly on the basis of triangular co-operation agreements with Western firms in which the Polish input is mainly from the construction industry. However, Poland's overall performance in the 1980s will, as in the 1970s, be strongly affected by the quality and price-competitiveness of the products offered and by its ability to provide good marketing and servicing facilities in the developed countries in particular. The Polish performance in these respects may be helped by improvements in the economic mechanism envisaged in the reform programme outlined in December 1980. But it will also depend on Poland's ability to continue to import substantial quantities of Western technology and equipment: already in the first half of the 1980s, much of the equipment imported in 1971-5 will be becoming obsolescent.

In principle it should not be quite as difficult for the Polish planners to hold the line on hard-currency imports as to achieve large growth in exports. A curtailment of investment was announced in the immediate aftermath of the 1980 strikes and the authorities were clearly hoping to alleviate some of the pressures on the economy (although this was to some extent a forced reaction to the impact of wage increases of approximately 10 per cent granted to buy off the strikers). Starting in the last quarter of 1980, Poland has been able to obtain short-term relief from her Comecon partners in the form of supplies of grain, other food-stuffs and consumer goods (mostly from the Soviet Union). The Soviet Union has promised aid of $1.1 billion in loans and $200 million in additional goods in 1981 (whether any or all of this is on a hard-currency basis is not clear). The USSR may decide to make further commitments to tide Poland over the particularly difficult two to three years ahead. Poland may also be able to cut back on hard-currency imports by expansion of normal trade with the Comecon countries, although in 1981 there will be an actual contraction of this trade. The current share of Poland's trade with Comecon is approximately 50 per cent, and although it was until fairly recently envisaged that trade with the Soviet bloc would increase somewhat less rapidly than trade with the West and the developing countries during 1981-5, this trend could now well be reversed. The figures for the first nine months of 1981 showed a small increase (3.1 per cent) in imports from the (Comecon) First Payment Area, in contrast to a drop in hard-currency imports of no less than 24.7 per cent.

In the short term, Poland has been at least equally successful in obtaining relief from the West. It was estimated in late 1981 that during 1981 Poland has obtained from Western official creditors about $2 billion in new export credits, to which could be added about another $2 billion of unutilized credits already in the pipeline. Food to a value of 600 million ECUs (approximately £357m) was obtained from the European Community at a substantial discount. This included 1.1 million tons of cereals. The United States also provided food aid. But it was obvious that Poland should not expect to rely indefinitely on such expedients.

Savings can be expected to be achieved by a reduction of non-essential imports from the West, for instance consumer goods. The area where the substitution will be distinctly more difficult is in imports of Western technology and industrial equipment. It seems unlikely that the Poles will wish to substantially curtail during the 1980s imports from the West of this type, which are, as mentioned above, crucial to Poland's export performance. Poland's cancellation in 1980 of a major project with the FRG, worth DM 2.5 billion for the construction of gas liquefication plants in order to produce methanol, was a sign of the gravity of the immediate crisis. But it should probably not be taken as an indication of likely Polish planning preferences in the medium term when presented with opportunities to acquire the benefits of Western technology backed by Western credits.

Probably the most important area where economic reform, complemented by a shift in investment priorities, might yield large benefits is that of agriculture. The agricultural sector has received a grossly inadequate investment for the past two decades. This has been especially marked in private agriculture (still accounting for over 70 per cent of all production). Government policies have discouraged initiative and have offered inadequate incentives to the private farmers, while state and collective farms have failed miserably to match the preferential investment treatment given them with corresponding gains in production. A typical comment on the failure of government policies is in the statistics for the yields achieved in growing sugar-beet, the production of which dropped from 14.2 million tons in 1979 to an estimated 10.5-11 million tons in 1980. Yields per acre were estimated to have dropped from 15.93 in 1950 to 10.6 in 1980.[6] At a time of extreme economic stringency, Poland is not now best placed to make a heavy shift of resources to the agricultural sector. But the need for a new approach appeared to be widely recognized in the aftermath of the strikes and by 1981 the government appeared determined to take drastic remedial action.[7]

The gravity of Poland's economic problems and the dilemma of those trying to introduce economic reforms was emphasized anew with the publication of the figures for the first nine months of 1981. These revealed that industrial production in September 1981 was running at a level 14 per cent lower than in September 1980, and that production was down 13.4 per cent on the first nine months of 1980. Supplies of meat were 25.8 per cent lower than in the comparable 1980 period while coal production was down by 19.1 per cent. Exports were 8.9 per cent lower. Meanwhile it was still impossible to assess the likely impact of economic reforms, since their final shape was not known. It seems likely that many of the features of the Hungarian economic system, including a measure of decentralization, the granting of greater scope for enterprise managers, and greater reliance on market mechanisms, will be adopted. What is much harder to predict at the time of writing is how far the reforms will move in a Yugoslav direction—that is, in allowing genuine self-management by workers. Demands by Solidarity for a major shift in this direction were, in late 1981, being (understandably) resisted by the authorities. The political ramifications of this issue are of course considerable, since they affect the very basis of the Nomenklatura system whereby the Party maintains close control over enterprises. In the more strictly economic sphere, the dilemma for the authorities is no less serious, since there is an obvious risk that workers' self-management could lead to an increase in the anarchic and centripetal tendencies so evident in Polish industry since August 1980. The argument for retaining a strong measure of central control in such circumstances could hardly be gainsaid.

Czechoslovakia

Czechoslovak spokesmen are placing increasing emphasis on the value of co-operation within Comecon, and it is expected that the share of trade with the socialist bloc will at least be maintained. In commenting on the performance of the Czechoslovak economy in 1976-80, Prime Minister Strougal stated that: 'it is noteworthy, and it corresponds entirely to our interests, that the share of trade and economic co-operation with Comecon countries rose from 66 per cent to 67.2 per cent this year [1980] over 1979'. In 1980/81, Czechoslovak leaders extolled in particular the benefits of trade with the USSR.

The most striking example of the price advantage of Czechoslovakia's dependence on Soviet raw materials is that, until 1984, Czechoslovakia benefits from a special credit with the Soviet Union which guarantees her annual shipment of five million tons of oil at the extremely low price of a mere $22.6 per ton. Although this represents only a little over a quarter of projected Czechoslovak imports, the remaining Czechoslovak oil requirement is supplied at the Comecon price which (in early 1981) was considerably below the world price. These price advantages, which are in repayment of credit extended to the USSR in 1966-74 in the form of deliveries of technical equipment and consumer goods, saved Czechoslovakia no less than $1.6 billion in her oil bill in 1980 alone (although against this must be set the fact that the USSR pays Comecon prices for imports of Czechoslovak products). Other raw materials which Czechoslovakia receives from the USSR at prices still below the world level are iron ore (84 per cent of imports in 1978), coal (57 per cent of imports) and cotton (67 per cent). Although the degree of Czechoslovakia's price advantage will substantially diminish as a result of the 1975 Moscow formula, which fixes prices according to a five-year moving average of world prices, the savings for Czechoslovakia up to 1984 will be particularly useful, thanks to the special terms negotiated for oil (assuming that the OPEC countries secure further large price increases).

Czechoslovakia's performance in supplying industrial products to the Comecon countries has not been without complaints. But Czechoslovakia's difficulties in meeting its orders to socialist countries were less serious than those in exporting to the West. Czechoslovak engineering exports, which constitute the main share of exports, both to socialist and to non-socialist countries, have failed to keep pace with what Trade Minister Barcak called 'the dynamic pace of world trade in engineering products and development'.[8] It was estimated in 1980 that only 1.8 per cent of Czech total industrial output was of a world standard.[9]

Another major advantage which the Czechoslovak leadership perceives in its emphasis on trading links with Comecon is the fact that Czechoslovakia has kept its foreign indebtedness to manageable proportions. Total foreign debt in late 1980 was estimated at only $4.4 billion, and the debt-service ratio at only 22 per cent (less than a quarter of that of Poland and the same percentage as Romania). If the Czechoslovak government wished this, they could expect to have somewhat less difficulty than either Poland or Romania in increasing the scale of their foreign borrowing during the 1980s. However, the readiness of Western lenders to grant further loans to any East European state has been impaired by the Polish experience. The present Czechoslovak leadership seems in any case likely to eschew this course: it is particularly sensitive to the political implications of dependence upon the West, and is determined to avoid allowing indebtedness to represent anything like a 'sword of Damocles' over its head comparable to that perceived to be hanging over Poland. The gravity of Poland's economic crisis as it deepened in 1981 will have reinforced such fears.

Czechoslovakia has committed itself to a number of long-term Comecon projects, of which the most substantial is the nuclear energy programme. Under this, Czechoslovakia is responsible for the production of Soviet-designed VVER-440 reactors for all of the European Comecon countries. Czechoslovakia is also making a major investment in the Khmelnitsky power station in the Ukraine (a sixth of the total cost of 1,500 million roubles), which in 1988-2003 will supply Czechoslovakia with 3,600 million kWh. The Czechoslovak construction of reactors will represent a heavy burden on the Czechoslovak engineering industry, which has suffered some dislocation as a result of the need to adjust rapidly to this new and technically challenging requirement. But the nuclear programme fits in well with the political and economic philosophy of the Czechoslovak leadership, and particularly with its patent preference for planning on a highly centralized and long-term basis, with the minimum of variables. In contrast to trade with the West, which is affected by a number of shifting and often unpredictable factors, the Czechoslovak share in the Comecon nuclear programme offers stability and assurance, even if at some cost. The aim is for nuclear power to cover in full increments in demand for electricity after 1980, with a target of meeting 30 per cent of demand by 1990 (15 per cent in 1985). Nuclear power will make a major contribution to the government's efforts to find ways of limiting imports of oil. However, the main impact may not come until the 1990s, when the importance of nuclear energy will be highlighted by the anticipated exhaustion (during that decade) of coal reserves in Northern Bohemia.[10]

Another major co-operative project in which Czechoslovakia is now involved is the Adria pipeline, which was planned to carry 250 million tons of Middle East oil a year to Czechoslovakia, Hungary and Poland.[11] The uncertainty of Iranian supplies leaves the volume of this source of supply much in doubt. Czechoslovakia has also contributed to the IGAT-II pipeline which was expected, under a deal with Irangas, to result in Soviet deliveries of natural gas to Czechoslovakia (from the Caucasus) in exchange for Iranian 'back-to-back' supplies to the Soviet Union. This is also now shrouded in uncertainty as a result of developments in Iran.

The major benefit Czechoslovakia derives from its strongly Comecon-directed trading and investment pattern can be summed up as stability and security. The main uncertainties in the present long-term co-operative projects derive not from Czechoslovakia's Comecon partners but from countries outside the bloc. But the prospects are not entirely rosy. Czechoslovak economic policy faces three main challenges: first, in the 1980s the Soviet Union will be no longer able to supply so high a proportion of Czechoslovakia's growing energy needs, as a result of which Czechoslovakia will increasingly have to look to other sources of supply; second, it will find difficulty in generating the currency earnings needed both to pay for growing imports of raw materials from outside the bloc and to maintain the present level of imports from the West, including technology and equipment required for the modernization of Czechoslovak industry; and third (although this would not be acknowledged as a weakness by Czechoslovakia's present leaders) Czechoslovakia's Comecon orientation will have the kind of side-effects on efficiency and production and on the satisfaction of consumer demands whose perception by an earlier generation of Czechoslovak planners in the 1960s led to the abortive reform experiment of 1968.

The first of these challenges is difficult to quantify. A plateau in Soviet oil deliveries has now been reached, with the Soviet Union committed only to maintaining, in 1981-5, the level of 19 million tons annually reached in 1980. While no estimates are currently available as to the expected growth in requirements for oil imports in 1981-5, it seems unlikely that this will be less than 4 to 5 per cent per annum, even allowing for considerable efforts by the authorities to achieve savings in consumption.[12] This could mean that by 1985 Czechoslovakia will need to import annually for hard currency something in the order of 5 million tons of oil, and it could well be more than this.

Similar considerations apply to the Czechoslovak requirement to import other raw materials. Czechoslovak planners are going on the assumption that the Soviet Union will maintain, but not significantly increase, supplies of other raw materials. The high level of Soviet supplies of natural gas (eight billion cubic metres estimated in 1980) is likely to be maintained or slightly increased. The Czechoslovak planners are aiming to raise production of indigenous fuels such as hard coal and lignite to achieve savings in 1981-5 of 10 million tons of solid fuel equivalent through the ambitious energy-saving scheme launched in 1979. The nuclear energy programme will, as seen, also make a significant contribution to the solution of energy needs, although the impact may be slight until 1983. Overall, the picture in 1985 may be that the much larger requirement for oil imports will be the only factor in the energy sector demanding substantial new outlays of hard currency. But imports of non-energy raw materials (for instance, rubber, aluminium) are likely to increase, and these will in many cases involve the expenditure of hard currency.

The need to increase hard-currency earnings in the 1980s presents for Czechoslovakia much the same problems as it does for Poland, with the difference that Czechoslovakia has to rely almost entirely on exports of manufactured products whereas the Poles export a substantial amount of raw materials. In the 1970s the Czechs encountered serious problems in selling their engineering goods in the West. These became acute after 1975 as Western countries moved into recession. But it was also caused by the low quality of many products (the estimate may be recalled that only 1.8 per cent of Czechoslovak products reach world standards) and by inadequate marketing and servicing facilities. Czechoslovak spokesmen have complained in strong terms about the effects of Western trade barriers and restrictions, including those of the EEC, while various complaints have been brought by Western manufacturers before the EEC of cases involving alleged dumping by Czechoslovakia.[13] The effects of various types of barrier in the non-communist world is virtually impossible to quantify, but they seem likely to be of less consequence than considerations of quality, effective marketing and servicing facilities.

In the 1980s, Czechoslovakia's ability to increase its exports will depend more than ever on the performance of its engineering sector: exports of wood, chemicals and consumer goods are expected to decrease because of growing domestic needs. Yet a certain lack of confidence is evident: in his report to the Eighteenth Session of the Central Committee,[14] Strougal mentioned that in drawing up the seventh five-year plan (for 1981-5) the majority of production units sounded failed to give a positive response when asked if they could fulfil the task of achieving a substantial growth of exports. Non-engineering areas which the Czechoslovaks hoped would achieve export growth are newspaper pulp, glass, ceramics and furniture. Somewhat belatedly, the Czechoslovak authorities are now also calling for greater international industrial co-operation agreements with both developed capitalist and Third-World countries (so far the number of such agreements is tiny). If Western countries move out of their recession in 1981, this will obviously help general export prospects. Overall, however, the outlook cannot be described as entirely promising.

What was known as the 'Set of Measures for the Improvement of the System of Planned Management of the Economy after 1980' came into full effect in 1981. This is designed to increase the efficiency of enterprises, by providing greater incentives for managers and employees, by demanding a more scrupulous application of financial principles including Soviet-style cost accounting (khozraschot) and by introducing penalties and rewards for improvement in *quality* as well as quantity. The price structure was also revised. The introduction of the full scheme was apparently to be accompanied by fairly radical changes in the price system, bringing this closer to world prices. The changes fall far short of a radical economic reform of the kind attempted in Hungary and (abortively) in Czechoslovakia in 1968: the market plays a minor role.

It fits very much into the category of administrative-type reform, which devolves only limited power to enterprises. The central planners will continue to be responsible for major investment (and foreign trade) decisions.

The Czechoslovak revision (the official avoidance of the word 'reform' is significant) bears a fairly close resemblance to Soviet practice and there is a parallel with the reform introduced in the Soviet Union in the summer of 1979. It is also fully compatible with the country's foreign trade needs and particularly the shape of its participation in joint projects with the Soviet Union and other Comecon countries. The large crash nuclear-engineering programme is, for example, one which is particularly suited to a highly centralized system of planning which is able to achieve rapid shifts of resources with little regard for market—or indeed social— forces. While it is claimed that the system will be beneficial in assisting the growth of Czechoslovakia's exports to developed capitalist countries, the improvement here may be rather limited. The main benefit could come from improved quality of some export products if this aspect of the change is successful.

In the 1970s the Czechoslovak regime governed by a combination of repressive measures against manifestations of dissent/opposition and the satisfaction of the material needs of a population which already enjoyed a relatively high standard of living within the bloc. Yet its performance in the latter respect appeared to be under considerable challenge by the end of the 1970s. The claimed increase in real personal consumption in the 1976-80 period was 10 per cent, that is 2 per cent annually. This compared with growth of real income of 4 per cent in 1971-2, and 2.6 per cent in 1975. The forecast for 1981/5 given in October 1980 in Strougal's report to the Central Committee was of a possible growth of average nominal income by only 1.8 per cent per year. This is a notably unambitious target and it suggests that the growth of consumption will be minimal. Significantly, in 1980 the Czechoslovak government was careful only to commit itself to maintaining rather than increasing the standard of living.

The failure to introduce decentralizing economic reforms is only one factor in Czechoslovakia's unimpressive economic performance. The striking deterioration in the 1970s of Czechoslovakia's terms of trade, and the difficulties deriving from both Western inflation and increasing competition at a time of recession, would have impeded economic growth under any form of economic management. However, the long-term problems of the Czechoslovak economy as reflected in, among other things, the lack of competitiveness of its products in Western markets, do appear to be connected with the lack of encouragement of initiative, and of the devolution of authority. For the 1980s, as in the 1950s, the regime seems to be pinning its faith on its ability to 'mobilize' the population to undertake hard and efficient work through ideologically based appeals. Although it can be claimed that this type of appeal produced results in the period of Czechoslovakia's extensive growth, in current circumstances it is far more questionable. In 1980 it was admitted that despite strong appeals for improvement, growth in productivity fell below target. At the same time the command economy seems ill-suited to achieve the efficient production and distribution of consumer goods in the 1980s any more than in the 1960s or 1970s. The existence of a strong 'parallel economy' is one manifestation of the problem, as is the phenomenon of state shops selling goods in short supply for hard currency. The failure to achieve an efficient system of distribution was well described by Vasil Bilak — Czechoslovakia's arch-dogmatist — when he stated (ironically, in the context of a diatribe directed principally at Western imperialists): 'The fact that Czechoslovakia produces a ton of steel per inhabitant is a great success. However, it has a small effect on someone who cannot buy a thing he badly needs: farmers' ploughs, citizens' scythes [sic], scissors, needles and hundreds of other so-called petty things.'

Romania

In the 1980s, the Romanian economy confronts more serious problems than in the 1970s, despite the fact that plans for the growth of national product are somewhat less ambitious than those of the last two decades. The problems stem partly from the fact that since the early 1970s Romania has become a net importer of energy resources. She will have to rely increasingly on imports of raw materials, and this in turn will augment the difficulty of holding imports to a level which will enable her to balance international payments. At the same time, like other bloc countries she is encountering increasing difficulties in exporting industrial goods to Western countries and, given the relatively high proportion of Romanian trade with non-socialist countries (53.5 per cent in 1978), this presents a more acute problem for Romania than it does for, say, Czechoslovakia. While Romania's indebtedness to the West was $8.38 billion in mid-1980, with a relatively low debt-service ratio, repayments will represent a continuing drain on the balance of payments, especially if a serious effort is made to work towards President Ceauşescu's stated goal of eliminating the whole of the Western debt by 1990.[15]

If Romania is able to fulfil her plans, she will have 'taken off' and become an industrialized country by 1990, with a per capita national income of $2,500, against $1,400 in 1976 (although these figures are probably underestimated and should be treated with caution). In 1981-5, the share of investment in national product will decline to 30 per cent from the exceptionally high figure of 33 per cent in 1976-80. But the growth rate, with its accompanying strain on resources, will remain high by current Comecon standards. The growth of gross industrial output is planned to be held at the 1976-80 level of 9-10 per cent per annum, with the growth of national income, however, falling to 6.7-7.4 per cent (against 9-10 per cent in 1976-80). Real income (social production) of the population (including the 'social wage') is expected to rise by 4.2-4.6 per cent per annum, and real wages by 3.0-3.4 per cent. The goal for 1990 is an increase in national income to no less than 250-280 per cent of the national income achieved in 1975.

The realization of these ambitious goals will depend heavily on Romania's ability to achieve further substantial growth in its trade. Some significant savings are expected through import substitution, while in the energy field the government has embarked on an ambitious programme to achieve conservation. Given that Romania uses three times as much energy to produce a given unit of production value as the average for EEC countries, the scope for savings is considerable, although the size will hinge on the degree of technological improvement and new investment in this sphere. But Romania's dependence on foreign trade is likely to remain considerable, with the export ratio at an estimated 28 per cent of GNP in 1990. Romania's development programme is predicated on the achievement of the tripling of foreign trade by 1990 over the level of 1975.

In its recent report on the Romanian economy, the World Bank identified three major challenges facing the Romanian economy.[16] These were:

(a) To increase economic efficiency in resource utilization and to improve product quality;

(b) to contain imports to a planned level to achieve sufficient export penetration of world markets for sustaining the targeted high growth rates;

(c) to develop the adaptability of the economic sectors to respond to world market changes and to offset the vulnerability of the economy to external economic oscillations.

While improvements in resource allocation can be achieved to some extent by the refinement of planning techniques, the problem of improving product quality may prove formidable, and this will have particularly important influences on export performance. Since the World Bank assessment was drafted, the Romanian government has introduced a 'New Economic Mechanism' which is designed to improve the efficiency by giving large production units rather greater scope for initiative, coupled with a new system of incentives designed to give workers and managers greater incentive to boost production and exports. The funds retained by production units, part of which was payable in incentives, were 2.6 times higher in 1979 than under the old system. A special bonus is provided for over-fulfilment of export tasks. This reform, introduced in March 1978, appears to have been implemented slowly and in mid-1980 Ceauşescu complained that it was even then 'poorly understood'. The reform provides, however, only a very limited degree of devolution of decision-making, and it is essentially an administrative type of reform, similar to the Czechoslovak 'Set of Measures'. Although the new incentives may have a certain influence in stimulating workers and management to meet production targets, the new Romanian model does not appear to make special provision for improvements in quality. While it was not possible, after its first eighteen months of operation, to make any definitive judgement about its likely impact, initial impressions were discouraging. In late 1980, the regime spoke of non-fulfilment of export targets and felt compelled to offer 'special bonuses' to workers for the production of crude oil, coal and iron ore.

The containment of imports may not be quite so difficult in the 1980s as the stimulation of exports in convertible currency. But the recent trends have not been encouraging. By 1980 it was apparent that the government was determined to restrict hard-currency imports, even in areas which were important for Romania's development, unless a counter-trade element could be incorporated into the deals. The government is committed to working for substantial savings in the use of energy. In 1976-80, it was hoped to achieve a reduction in the order of 20-23 per cent. The government's goal is to achieve self-sufficiency in energy by 1990, with the extensive development of nuclear and hydro-electric energy. However, most of the benefits will accrue only after 1985; in the first half of the 1980s, the import requirements for energy and other raw materials will remain heavy and a substantial part of this will only be obtainable for hard currency.

Exports are planned to grow at a rate of 6-7 per cent per annum between 1981 and 1990. While this is a lower rate than in 1976–80 (12–13 per cent), its achievement may not be easy. The penetration of Western markets is likely to prove particularly difficult, even allowing for an upturn in economic activity in the EEC countries after 1981 and for some further relaxation in restrictions applying to the sale of Romanian products in EEC countries. The sober assessment in the World Bank's 1979 Report is likely to hold good for some time: 'While Romania has made an inroad into the convertible markets, it is likely to be an uphill task to increase or even to maintain its stake.'[17]

The still highly centralized Romanian economy is not very well equipped to display the flexibility needed to withstand oscillations in the world economy (the third point of those quoted above in the World

Bank Report). Short of major reforms in the economic system, of which there is so far little sign, this is not a challenge which can easily be surmounted. The Romanians have, however, been implementing a revision of the producer price structure which they describe as being designed to make the economy more responsive to changes in international trade. They have also introduced an exchange rate reform designed to encourage hard-currency exports and Comecon imports. Chemicals and machinery are important areas of Romanian exports which are peculiarly sensitive to fluctuations in world trade. One effect of this dilemma may be to increase Romanian interest in the relatively more stable Comecon markets on a basis of long-term agreements.

A shift in Romanian thinking about the relative attractions of Western and Eastern markets was detectable in the course of 1980 and became even more marked in 1981. At the Thirty-fourth Session of Comecon in May 1980, Romania surprised some observers by taking a lead in criticizing failures to move sufficiently quickly in effecting joint planning and agreement on co-operative ventures amongst the members. In late 1980 and in 1981, Romanian Ministers laid increasing stress on the benefits of economic co-operation with Comecon countries.

Although Romania may continue to see political advantage in maintaining a high level of trade with the developed West, it could well be that the proportion of this trade in Romanian total trade will diminish somewhat during the 1980s. Romania may be increasingly attracted by the advantages of increasing further its trade with the developing countries (which in 1978 accounted for approximately 20 per cent of its total trade). The Romanians may see scope for increasing the number of co-operation agreements with developing countries, sometimes in co-operation with Western firms. Many of these countries offer less daunting export markets for industrial products than the developed West. However, the OPEC countries, to whom Romania will be looking for imports of oil, have become increasingly choosy with regard to their purchases and are likely in most cases to demand payment for oil exports either in hard currency or in sought-after products (such as meat) which are regarded as roughly equivalent.

If, as seems likely, Romania pays increasing attention to trading and investment opportunities in Comecon and the developing world, the impact may be more medium- to long-term than immediate. In the early 1980s, the preoccupation of the Romanian authorities about hard-currency requirements is unlikely to diminish, and some difficult decisions will have to be taken about the level of imports of capital goods and industrial products which can only be obtained in the developed West. One of the options open to the Romanians would be to resort to fresh borrowings in the West rather than to carry through with the stated policy of eliminating the foreign debt by the end of the decade. Such a temptation certainly exists, and it would not be altogether surprising if the 1990 target was allowed to slip. However, the situation as it had developed by late 1981 was far from encouraging in so far as prospects for fresh borrowings were concerned. The Romanians were reported to have confronted serious problems in meeting hard-currency obligations in November/December 1981, and to have sought a restructuring of their debts to a number of major Western banks as a palliative. This was in addition to a $1.48 billion loan obtained (against some fairly stringent conditions) from the IMF in June 1981.

One factor which may help to inhibit any Romanian leadership in the 1980s from greatly reducing economic links with the developed West may be the perceived benefit of trade with the West for developing consumer-goods industries in Romania. So far rather little attention has been paid to consumer needs, but there were signs in 1980 (partly in connection with events in Poland) that the leaders were becoming increasingly aware of the desirability of doing more to provide durable consumer goods as well as an adequate supply of food to the population. The plan for 1981 provided only for a 2.5 per cent increase in the production of consumer goods, and Romanian plans for subsequent years are unclear. If this production is thereafter to be substantially increased, the Romanians would in most cases be better served if they were to import equipment for new factories from the West in preference to the Comecon East.

Prospects for trade with the West

Poland, Czechoslovakia and Romania all entered the 1980s with an enhanced awareness of the advantages of trade and investment within Comecon and of economic links with the Soviet Union, particularly in terms of the greater stability these offered compared with the volatile markets of the West. The Czechoslovak leaders claimed this as a vindication of the strongly Comecon-oriented policies they have been pursuing consistently since 1969. For Poland and Romania, however, the implications were less clear-cut. Both countries continued to see benefit in maintaining a high level of trade with the West and with developing countries. In the case of Poland, this was partly a direct consequence of the decision to import Western investment goods taken at the beginning of the 1970s. The accumulation of a massive scale of debt has made it imperative for Poland to attempt in the 1980s to increase the level of its hard-currency exports and this in turn depends, albeit to a somewhat lesser extent than in the early 1970s, on the continued import of technology and advanced industrial equipment from the West. Few of the investment goods Poland needs to increase exports in competitive world markets could be substituted from Eastern sources. Romania, with a more manageable debt, had rather greater freedom of manoeuvre. The economic advantages for Romania of increased links with Comecon countries were indisputable in the field of energy. However, the leadership must have been aware of the risk that a marked increase in economic dependence on the Soviet Union or a radical impulse to Comecon integration on the lines first advocated by Khrushchev could have adverse consequences for Romania's ability to pursue an autonomous foreign policy.

Assuming that the Czechoslovak government continues its present policies, it should be possible in principle to achieve balanced trade with the West in 1981-5 and probably to achieve also some reduction in the level of indebtedness during this period. For Poland and Romania the problem of balancing accounts with the West by 1985 is more acute. A study by the Austrian Federal Ministry of Commerce, Trade and Industry undertaken in 1978 has established that if all East European countries were to try to balance their trade with the West by 1985, this would mean acceptance of an extremely low level of 1.7-2.9 per cent growth of imports from the West during that period, together with a vastly increased level of imports from within Comecon. The relative stagnation of imports would need to be accompanied by a substantial growth of exports to OECD of 6.7–7.9 per cent.[18] In the view of the authors of the study, such a target would be exceedingly difficult to meet, given (a) that possibilities for import substitution within Comecon were in practice very limited, and (b) that OECD countries were unlikely to reconcile themselves over a long period of time to accepting a substantial growth in penetration of their markets by goods from Comecon countries while their own exports to Comecon stagnated. The study argued that the most favourable solution for both East and West would be a balancing of trade by the 1990s, which would allow a substantial increase of Eastern imports as well as of exports from the West, although this would depend on a number of conditions, such as the avoidance of increased protection in OECD markets and the willingness of Western banks and governments to extend further loans and credits.

The prospects of countries like Poland and Romania earning substantially greater hard currency would certainly be improved if a breakthrough were to be achieved in negotiations between the EEC and Comecon for an agreement between the two organizations. But, in the shorter term, prospects for trade will probably be influenced more by the economic growth prospects of individual EEC countries and their need to take measures to protect employment than by the establishment of such a formal link. If, as seems likely, unemployment recedes only very gradually in EEC and OECD countries, this will inevitably limit the prospects for growth in Comecon exports.

If Comecon countries were finally, in the course of the 1980s, to take the plunge and attempt to introduce currency convertibility, this would improve the conditions for East–West trade. The Hungarians and Romanians have already stated officially that convertibility is their goal, and others, for instance the Poles, entertain similar hopes. But the early effects of convertibility would probably rather take the form of greater rationality of planning within Comecon than of shifts in the actual pattern of East–East and East–West trade. It must in any case be remembered that a portion of trade between Comecon countries (estimated at 10–20 per cent) is conducted in hard currency and therefore already 'convertible.'

Political implications of economic links with the West

Economic links with the West would appear to have had, generally speaking, only a small influence on the direction of domestic economic policies in the states surveyed. The influence exerted has worked in two directions. In Czechoslovakia it can be argued that the attempt at limited economic reform in 1980/81, as well as the much more ambitious but abortive reforms of the 1960s, were influenced by the need to develop an industry better able to compete in Western markets. But this would appear to be less important, at least insofar as the present reforms are concerned, than the perceived need to satisfy consumer expectations: for all the puritanism of the dogmatists such as Bilak the government cannot afford to ignore the material basis of its social compact with the populace.

In Poland, economic links with the West had arguably the opposite effect of allowing the Gierek regime to govern without carrying through any substantial economic reform. At the beginning of the 1970s, the regime turned to the West for credits and investment as an alternative to the implications of a radical price reform (which the 1970 strikes and demonstrations had shown to be politically unacceptable). But it would be wrong to deduce from this that Western investment *caused* the collapse of reform. The fundamental explanation lies in the fact that (in part because of the lack of trust of much of the population, including most workers) the Polish government felt too weak to apply drastic and painful remedies. A secondary explanation is that when reform was hesitantly attempted in 1972-3, it was doomed to failure because of the overheating of the economy and the absence of the 'slack' required for a successful reform. As Dr Brus has opined, economic reform was never given a proper chance in Poland - nor indeed elsewhere in Eastern Europe.[19]

East European regimes have generally appeared to be sensitive to the political implications of increased economic links with the West. As has been seen in earlier chapters of this study, Romania in particular has appeared to pursue a deliberate policy of expanding links with the capitalist world and the Third World as a counterbalance to the influence of the Soviet Union: this has indeed been a key element in the assertion of an 'autonomous' foreign policy. In 1980/81, however, the leadership showed that if such a policy came into conflict with what were perceived as the vital economic needs of the state, it could be moderated or reversed with little apology. Although the recent evidence of a shift towards Comecon is an insufficient basis for confident generalization, it would certainly seem that Ceauşescu has a healthy sense of realism in the area of foreign policy when confronted with severe economic problems. The Czechoslovak example shows a close correlation between the regime's political aims and the degree of permitted dependence on trade with the West. The only serious anomaly is the perception of at least the pragmatists in the government (for example Strougal and Barcak) that trade with the West can assist the meeting of consumer expectations, a requirement which seems likely to assume increasing importance in the context of a 'social compact' between regime and people.

The Polish example is more complicated. If the early years of the Gomulka regime are excepted, the Polish government has seen trade with the West much less in terms of political benefit than of economic advantage. The decision of the Gierek-directed 'technocrats' to turn to the West for investment resources was determined above all by the hope that external assistance would generate economic growth sufficient to satisfy the expectations of ordinary Poles — and especially of workers. The fact that Western banks were replete with funds was, of course, highly relevant. Had the resources been available in the East, this would doubtless have been seen as carrying lesser risks. The main political repercussions of the turning to the West were in making the regime more conscious of its external image. Although this is something which it is impossible to quantify, it would certainly appear that Gierek's interest in obtaining credits and investment from the West had a significant influence on his conduct of internal policy. As the analysis in Chapter 6 suggests, the regime's interest in maintaining a relatively 'liberal' image is likely to have had some impact on its policy towards dissent and opposition. This stood in marked contrast to the attitude of the Czechoslovak government, which paid remarkably little heed to outside (or, at any rate, non-Soviet) opinion. It would, however, be misleading to conclude that the tolerance of the Polish authorities in the 1970s was determined exclusively, or even largely, by external concerns. A more realistic perspective is that the Gierek regime was, to a greater extent than the regime of Gomulka post-1959, acutely conscious of the need to win popular support, and that it was aware that repressive policies would detract from this. The development of more normal relations with the West was also a means towards acceptance at home. The decision to invite the Pope to Poland in 1979 was important, less in terms of the regime's wish to maintain a good international image (though this aspect was certainly not without significance), than in terms of acknowledgement of its own vulnerability before public opinion: the riots of 1976 had dramatically demonstrated the strength of latent popular dissatisfaction, notwithstanding the huge wage rises of 1971-5.

As has been noted, the scale of indebtedness of Czechoslovakia has so far been of manageable proportions and seems likely to remain so in the foreseeable future. As the reader hardly needs reminding, the scale of Poland's debts is of quite a different order, and the political implications are highly significant. The effect of the acute Polish economic crisis of 1980-81 was to make the Polish government still more dependent on both Western and Comecon support. The weakness of the Polish government's position was perceived in Moscow as carrying domestic political risks, but it was probably not seen as carrying risks in the sphere of foreign policy, since dependence on the West was more than balanced by increased dependence on Soviet support. The highly conformist foreign policy pursued by the Polish government during the crisis was but one indication of this.

The Polish government benefited from the fact that Western governments, and also a majority of Western bankers, perceived an interest in preventing the collapse of the Polish economy. This was partly to protect the large Western investment in Poland, but governments were also influenced by wider political concerns: a collapse of the economy, and of the Polish authorities' ability to control events, risked creating a larger crisis affecting Western security and the totality of East–West relations. This theme is discussed further in Chapter 7.

In the 1981 debate about the rescheduling and/or refinancing of Poland's debts, suggestions were put forward that one of the conditions to be demanded by banks should be the imposition of IMF-type controls, including the monitoring of Polish economic policy. In the event, these ideas were not pressed home. The discussions amongst Western creditors demonstrated, however, that although Western governments or banks had only limited scope to influence directly economic or other policy in a bloc state, their views could have a certain relevance.[20] The Polish authorities were clearly sensitive to the advantages of winning at least the tacit approval of Western circles for their economic policies, and appeared to pay heed to Western belief in the urgent need for economic reform. This must, however, be seen in perspective: when, for example, the Polish authorities were elaborating plans for economic reform in the spring and summer of 1981, it appeared that they were more concerned about pressures emanating from Solidarity than about likely Western reactions.

In the economic sphere, the Polish crisis illustrated, above all, the extent to which the Soviet Union and the West have come to share common interests in Eastern Europe. It has been assumed by some Western bankers that, in the event of a bloc state being forced to default on the repayment of its debts, the Soviet Union would step into the breach and meet the payment (the so-called 'umbrella theory'). The Polish experience has suggested that reality is more complicated, and that the USSR will go to some lengths to avoid being placed in such a position. In the event, the Soviet sacrifice was limited to deferment of repayment of loans to the Soviet Union until after 1985 (a concession announced in August 1981), with Western banks and governments bearing the burden of the rescheduling of Poland's debts to the West.

6 The competing pulls: the internal political scene

How are the political systems of Eastern Europe responding to the competing influence of the Soviet Union on the one hand and the West on the other? To what extent are the present challenges to internal stability in Eastern Europe the product of internal strains, and how far are they externally induced?

The country which has self-evidently been subject to the greatest recent strain is Poland. Since 1956 there have been frequent shifts in the internal orientation of the Polish regime. But its orientation towards the outside world has shown a rough consistency. Poland is today, as it was in the late 1950s, the Eastern bloc country which (with the possible exception of Hungary) is the most open to contact with the West and which allows the greatest freedom of movement. While Gomulka's regime in the 1960s belied the promise of its early years, the successive regimes of Gierek and Kania have accepted that an opening to the West, at least in terms of controlled political and human interchange, is desirable in order to balance the realities of Poland's position in the Eastern bloc with its strong Western cultural and historical affinities. One result of increased exposure has been that ordinary Poles have come to identify to a yet greater degree with Western values in such disparate matters as dress and their attitude to authority. The government's aim has been to try to ensure that this exposure, while serving as a safety-valve, does not interfere with the essential features of the political system and with Poland's alliances with the Soviet Union and other bloc members.

The major political crises in the recent past have been those sparked by student disturbance in March 1968; the workers' strike and riots of

79

December 1970; the debate over the revision of the Constitution in 1975; the riots of June 1976; and the wave of strikes which paralysed Poland in the summer and early autumn of 1980. It may be useful to examine how far, in each of these cases, external influences played a part. The concept of 'external influence' here used is the broad one of the extent to which the attraction of Western values, in their widest definition, has affected internal political developments. It also covers the only indirectly related repercussions of changes in external relations and in the external environment.

The student disturbances of 1968 were a reflection of the gap separating the Gomulka regime's theoretical dedication to the pursuit of a 'Polish way' to socialism and the reality of its increasingly repressive internal policies. The university students were rebelling against an educational system which stifled originality and innovation, and which denied Poland's traditional cultural values. A poll taken at this time showed that only one student in two considered himself to be a Marxist.[1] Many of those who did see themselves as Leftists believed—not unlike the French students who rebelled against their system later in the same year—that the existing system discouraged self-expression and freedom of thought. One of the latter category was Jacek Kuron, later the leader of KOR, who declared at the time: 'I want to tell you what a communist is. A communist is a man who fights for social justice, for freedom and equality, for socialism. He goes to prison for years because of his beliefs and activities and, once released, he again undertakes his revolutionary activities. This ideal of a communist should be the guiding beacon of your lives.'[2] The tough measures adopted by the government against the students, a large number of whom were arrested, left a bitter taste which had its influence on later developments.

There was no direct connection between the Polish student troubles and outside developments. The fact that this upsurge of student rebelliousness almost coincided with the major period of student unrest in the West appears to have been largely fortuitous; certainly there is no evidence of which the author is aware to suggest a direct causal connection. The one external event which did have some influence was the Six Day Arab-Israeli War of 1967: the Polish government's slavish support for the Arab cause, in deference to the Soviet Union, estranged many Polish intellectuals. However, the main cause of the student unrest would appear to have been an internally generated exasperation with an educational and political system which stifled originality of thought and creativity.

The repression of students was followed by still more repressive policies, promoted by a faction within the party and bureaucracy (General Moczar's), against intellectuals whose loyalty was suspect. Jews were persecuted for alleged Zionist sympathies in the wake of the 1967 Arab-Israeli War, and large numbers of the best-educated Poles —including many whose hopes that the communist system could be reformed from within were dashed by the course of events in Czechoslovakia—went into exile in 1968-70. Apart from the effects of the collapse of reform in Czechoslovakia, this emigration was influenced by what was perceived as an increasingly narrow and dogmatic outlook on the part of Gomulka himself, and also of strongly anti-Semitic and anti-intellectual elements within the party, epitomized by General Moczar, whose star appeared to be in the ascendant.

Attention has been drawn by various writers to the curious coincidence between the December 1970 strikes and disturbances on the Baltic seaboard and the signature of the Polish—West German Treaty which took place just two months earlier. In this case the connection lies mainly in the conclusion apparently drawn by the Polish government that signature of the Treaty would serve to consolidate its moral authority in other spheres: the government was aware that a majority of Poles welcomed the Treaty, seeing it as a success for the regime's diplomacy and betokening the further easing of contacts with the West. At a deeper level, Poles felt a sense of emotional release as a result of the guarantee now finally given of their state's territorial integrity in the wake of four partitions. It is suggested that awareness of the credit thus gained helped to bolster the government's confidence that increases in the prices of meat and basic foodstuffs would be accepted by the population as unavoidable. However, while such considerations may have had a certain influence on the non-conformist as well as on the conformist intelligentsia, they would appear to have had minimal influence on Polish workers. The violent reaction to the announcement of price rises demonstrated the workers' overriding preoccupation with material concerns and their strongly felt disillusionment with the government's performance in raising their living standards (which had increased by a total of only 8 per cent in 1965-70). The intelligentsia, traumatized by the events of 1968, played no part in the 1970 disturbances, adopting what has been described as a 'neutral' attitude,[3] though many intellectuals did not conceal their pleasure when these resulted in the demise of the anti-intellectual Gomulka regime.

The entirely working-class character of the protest movement of December 1970 was testimony to the emerging militancy of Polish workers and to their capacity for self-organization. The intensity of this protest may also have been connected with social origin: the majority of the workers were of peasant stock, having left the land only in the post-war era. This arguably contributed to their distrust for authority and their preoccupation with securing a higher standard of living.

The minor crisis which arose over the government's proposed revision of the Polish constitution in 1975-6 was by contrast clearly affected by changes in the international environment. The government's desire to proclaim Poland a 'socialist' state was in part a belated recognition that Poland was lagging behind the other East European states, all of whom had already produced new constitutions announcing their transformation from the stage of 'people's democracies' into fully 'socialist' states. It may also have been calculated to impress the Soviet Union with the ideological rectitude of Poland's leaders at a time when the balance of the country's trade had shifted dramatically towards the West; while there is no direct evidence of pressure exercised by the Soviet Union, this may well have been a contributory factor. Although, in the Soviet and PUWP calculation, the constitutional requirement may have seemed little more than a formality it is worth noting that, in the Polish national tradition, constitutions have had a special place, for instance the '3 May Constitution'.

The proposed amendments enshrined the leading role of the communist party, and the permanence of the alliance with the Soviet Union by asserting an 'unshakeable fraternal bond' with that country; they also defined citizens' rights by making them contingent on the fulfilment of duties to the state. The proposals encountered a degree of protest from opposition groups and from the Catholic hierarchy, which had not been foreseen by the regime. Compromise formulations were eventually accepted in which the government gave ground on the issue of citizens' rights and also accepted a less controversial formulation of the link with the Soviet Union. On the issue of the leading role of the party, no ground was given: the party was described as the 'leading political force in society in the construction of socialism'.

Those who were disposed to criticize the clumsy form of the government's handling of the proposed revision derived encouragement from the progress of detente and from the signature of the Helsinki Final Act in August 1975. The Final Act, while not of course precluding alliances, laid stress on the principles of sovereignty and equality of nations. It also sanctified the right of any nation to opt for neutrality if it so wished. The assertion of an 'unshakeable' bond with the Soviet Union, while not an inaccurate description of past reality, was hardly fully concordant with the spirit of Helsinki. The Final Act's formulation on human rights (Principle VII) was also a source of moral encouragement: Principle VII presented human rights as absolute and there was no suggestion that they should be regarded as contingent on the fulfilment of duties to the state. More important than any legal considerations was the general atmosphere engendered by detente and the CSCE process. The Polish government's close and enthusiastic identification with this process was a factor which could not be separated from its desire to give proof of ideological orthodoxy. The net result of this troublesome exercise in amending the Constitution was to demonstrate the vulnerability of the government to the forces of critical opinion at a time of 'mature détente'. Its tactical retreat encouraged its opponents and was one of the factors which led to the formation of organized opposition groups in 1976-7.

The other, still more important catalyst provoking the emergence of organized opposition was the second bout of workers' disturbances in June 1976. The disturbances themselves had little connection with external events: they were a spontaneous emotional response to the announcement of rises in food prices which workers believed to threaten the maintenance of their living standards. They were also, like the 1970 strikes, a protest against the fact that the working masses had virtually no influence over government policy, given that the political system made no allowance for effective participation from below. The disturbances were not co-ordinated and there is no evidence of manipulation by opposition elements amongst the intelligentsia. However, the government's brutal treatment of the ring leaders and other activists had the important result of stirring the intellectuals to rally to the defence of workers: the formation of the Workers' Defence Committee (KOR) in September 1976 represented the first attempt at an organized link between intellectuals and workers in Poland. KOR's major early achievement was its successful defence of arrested workers and the securing of their release.[4] KOR's links with workers were continued when KOR offered assistance in the editing of the workers' journal *Robotnik* which championed labour rights, including the right to form free trade unions. This was followed by the formation of other groups which were rather less broadly based. The first of these to be established, the Movement for the Defence of Human and Civil Rights (ROPCiO) (1977), adopted a more rightward stance than that of KOR, favouring a democratization of the political system along Western parliamentary lines. Its philosophy, which emphasized social factors, had much in common with Christian Democracy, for instance in the FRG. Later, one of the founders of the ROPCiO, Leszek Moczulski, set up the overtly nationalist and right-wing Confederation of Independent Poland (PPN) (1979), with a secret membership, whose goals include the achievement of independence from the Soviet Union. The distinction between KOR and the other groups went further than the usual Left-Right dichotomy. While the general tendency in the somewhat loose collection of individuals comprising KOR could probably best be described as in the direction of social democracy, it was also unique in eschewing a political programme as such: unlike PPN which had clear political objectives, KOR and its successor KSS ('KOR') (Social Self-Defence Committee 'KOR') aimed to enlarge gradually the area for autonomous social self-expression by encouraging groups in society to take initiatives independent of party and government. Its outlook has been summarized thus: 'We don't expect free elections, abolition of censorship and of political police;

free Poland remains in dreamland, but the margin of possible reforms and of reforms which will progressively transform the relationship between society and power is not negligible.'[5]

The wave of strikes in July–September 1980 bore a number of close resemblances to the disturbances of 1970 and 1976. The important difference, however, is that in 1980 Polish workers for the first time pressed for direct access to the political system, in order to make a positive impact on it, and to contribute to the shaping of policy; earlier, their aims were interdictory only. The workers in the Baltic cities were expressing a form of alienation: for too long they had been ignored by the communist party and they resented the contemptuous treatment accorded them by party functionaries and bureaucrats. The events of 1970 had also left a powerful after-taste of bitterness. As was well publicized in the Western press at the time, the Gdansk and Szczecin strike committees included in their demands not only the right to form independent trade unions but also the lifting of censorship regarding the negotiation of their claims, permission for Church sermons to be broadcast, and the release of arrested dissidents. 1980 was also different in the sense that, although there is no evidence that KSS ('KOR') or other opposition groups either instigated the strikes or played a more substantial role in their co-ordination than that of ensuring the circulation of objective information, the strike committees made substantial use of opposition talent, especially from KOR and Catholic reformist intellectuals during the negotiations. Both Catholic intellectuals and KOR played an important role in advising the incipient 'free' unions how to draft statutes with a view to securing registration. They also gave tactical advice concerning the management of the inevitable trials of strength with the powerful forces in the Polish governmental and judicial apparatus opposed to reform.

As the 1980 Polish crisis progressed, official attacks on the allegedly disruptive activities of 'anti-socialist forces' gained in intensity. Not surprisingly KSS ('KOR'), as well as the more rightward-leaning groups, was included. The official media drew attention to what were claimed to be links between KOR and counter-revolutionary subversive centres in the West. It was said that KOR has been founded not in Poland but at a secret meeting in Geneva in May 1975 (that is, before the 1976 riots) where dissidents 'of various kinds' were promised funds from subversive centres in order to promote human rights causes against the Polish government.[6]

However, so far as this writer is aware, no hard evidence has been adduced to support this allegation. All the indications are that KOR was formed in Poland as an *ad hoc* response to injustices perpetrated during and after the 1976 disturbances. So far as Western connections are concerned, the sensitivity of the Polish authorities may partly reflect the degree of success KOR obtained in gaining publicity and expressions of sympathy in Western Europe. The most valuable achievement was probably in winning the support of Eurocommunists: a letter by Kuron to Enrico Berlinguer pleading the KOR case regarding the post-June 1976 persecutions was published in *L'Unita* and evoked a sympathetic response on the part of the PCI. Publicity was also given in *Der Spiegel*, while contact groups were set up in a number of West European capitals. When Kuron, Michnik and other KOR members were arrested in the spring of 1977, FRG Young Socialists made an appeal for their release 'in the spirit of Helsinki'; when a general amnesty was declared on the Polish National Day – 22 July 1977– this was acclaimed by Western media as an act of political realism.[7] There was no evidence of funding of KOR from the West. The specific charge[8] that 'the technical resources used for printing and publication activities were supplied ... from abroad' may refer to limited help the unofficial publishing house 'Nowa'(which has printed a number of KOR documents) has been given by sympathizers in the West. It seems reasonable to conclude that the main benefit accruing to KOR from the West came mainly in the form of moral support. The fact that Western communist and socialist parties lent support of this kind was particularly welcome to it.

A key factor which led to the explosion of 1980 was growing awareness of the bankruptcy of the Gierek government's management of the economy, and the final descrediting of the authorities' 'Propaganda of success'. There were, however, a number of ways in which the external environment may also be said to have played a part, both in strengthening the resolve of Polish workers to take action and in influencing the authorities to seek a political solution rather than a trial of strength. There was, first, the stimulus which the Final Act gave to dissenting groups in Poland, including most notably KOR, in pressing for the observance of basic human rights and trade union rights. Second, the election of Cardinal Wojtylat as Pope, and his visit as Pope to Poland in 1979, was a source of moral encouragement to those who believed that there was scope for reducing the area of direct control by the state and for enlarging the area of democratic freedoms. It boosted the confidence of Poles who believed that Poland's historical traditions justified the stronger assertion of specifically Polish solutions to the nation's problems. The Pope's visit was organized with only minimal assistance from the authorities, and it appears to have brought home vividly to many Poles the irrelevance of much of the communist system: their shared national values were seen to be more important. Moreover, the visit showed how easy it was to co-operate on practical matters without reference to political jargon. The Pope's own frank and direct style of addressing problems contributed to this awakening. Last but not least, the visit boosted the authority of the Church. While in 1980 the Church was not the instigator of change, union organizers including especially Walesa regarded it as a source of inspiration and support; the help provided by Catholics close to Cardinal Wyszynski was also of practical benefit — arguably equal to that supplied by KOR. Third (although the causal nexus is more difficult to establish), increasing contact with the West had the effect of weakening further the confidence of ordinary Poles in the efficiency of the communist economic system. When, for example, expensive new Western plant was imported into Poland, to be brought into operation only after long delays and then utilized at well below its capacity, it became obvious to Polish workers that the system was inefficient.[9] Comparisons with Western standards of living were widely known. Although Lech Walesa was little travelled, he and other Solidarity organizers were well aware of the comparison between Polish living standards and those in leading Western countries.[10]

A fourth factor was the Polish government's own stake in détente as reflected, for instance, in the westward shift of trade policy, and in the steadily increasing governmental exchanges with the West. This cut two ways. Gierek's personal success in cultivating ties with top Western leaders was arguably a negative factor in the conduct of internal policy: the deference shown to him, and the sympathy with which the Polish government as well as people was evidently viewed in many Western quarters, may well have contributed to the leadership's exaggerated confidence in its ability to cope with problems at home. At the same time the fact of Poland's extensive economic ties with the West could not be entirely divorced from the regime's conduct of internal policy: Poland's good image in the West was linked with its government's reputation as being relatively 'liberal' by East European standards, and with the proof it had given of genuine progress in the implementation of the Final Act (in facilitating human contacts and in tolerating, even if not sanctioning, a degree of freedom of expression). By contrast with Czechoslovakia, the Polish regime was in fact remarkably tolerant of dissenting opinion, for instance as expressed in the burgeoning *samizdat* publications. While it would be an over-simplification to suggest that external factors were alone responsible for the regime's relative tolerance of opposition (the regime's realization of its political weakness is likely to have been equally important in the post-1976 period), it must surely have been a significant factor.

There was nothing to suggest that the attitude of strikers towards the Soviet Union was any different in 1980 from that in 1970 and 1976: in all three Polish crises it was obvious to all that the Soviet factor was vitally important and that, if certain limits were overstepped, the Brezhnev Doctrine might be invoked. The implications of the Soviet invasion of Afghanistan were twofold. On the one hand it re-emphasized the Soviet Union's readiness to use force to preserve a 'gain of socialism' if other methods failed; on the other hand, the strength of Western and non-aligned reaction highlighted the political costs of the military option, and the strong Soviet incentive for trying to find non-military solutions in future similar contingencies.

Czechoslovakia

Developments in Czechoslovakia have represented an almost perfect counterpoint to developments in Poland. As we have seen, the regime has sought deliberately to insulate itself from outside influences. This has produced a semblance of stability. The purged Czechoslovak Communist Party leadership has held together and has suffered few significant changes in the past decade. There have been no large-scale disturbances and even minor manifestations of unrest have been rare. Czechoslovak workers have, despite disappointingly low increments in their real earnings, maintained discipline and at least the appearance of dedication to work. The government has been careful to ensure that the level of its foreign borrowings should not rise to a level which might affect its internal freedom (as noted in Chapter 5). The leadership enters the 1980s apparently still more firmly committed to a policy of close reliance on the Soviet Union in both the political and the economic fields.

The external implications of the policy of insulation have already been covered. In the internal political field the regime faces two main challenges. The first is that it is inevitably difficult to exclude values and ideas emanating from the West in an era of mass communication and at a time when greater contacts at all levels between Eastern and Western Europe are enjoined in the Final Act. Vasil Bilak recognized this problem when, in a report to the Fifteenth Session of the Communist Party Central Committee in March 1980, he pointed out that with growing technical sophistication Czechoslovakia would become more, not less, exposed to foreign broadcasts and television transmissions. In the same report he coupled a reference to the positive aspects of tourism with a warning to all Czechoslovaks who came into close contact with foreign tourists to be always aware of being citizens of a socialist state and to behave accordingly.[11] The antidote of Bilak and other typically hardline members of the communist party leadership is to urge a return to original socialist values and the eschewal of the 'consumerism' of the West. This puritanical form of communism is, however, at some variance not only with trends in the West, but also with trends in other East European countries including Hungary and the spirit of 'renewal' in Poland. It may also be wondered how far even the hardliners believe in this type of rhetoric: it has in practice for many years not been evident that consumerism is a main instrument of the legitimation of East European regimes.

The second challenge stems from the regime's disappointing recent performance in improving the efficiency of the economy and in raising living standards: as noted in Chapter 5, real wages are believed to have dropped in 1979 and at best stagnated in 1980, while the outlook is not particularly promising. Even the most puritanical hardliners acknowledge that the party's and government's standing are affected by such fundamental bread-and-butter issues. One effect of this is to make the less dogmatically inclined Czechoslovak planners and managers more aware of the advantage of trade and economic co-operation with the West, which offers one means of overcoming the obstacles to improved industrial efficiency and a resumption of growth in real incomes. A second possible effect is to make them more receptive to arguments in favour of radical economic reform, notwithstanding the political risks which conservatives have believed this to carry. As yet, however, there is no clear sign of such a tendency emerging. Insofar as any clear tendency was observable in 1980-81, the emphasis was on the need for discipline.

The major recent manifestations of the first of these challenges have been the emergence of Charter 77 at the beginning of 1977 and of its offshoot, the Committee for the Unjustly Prosecuted (VONS) which was formed in 1978. In part, the Charter reflected the recognition that direct confrontation with the Husák government was not a practical possibility: in the wake of the 1968-9 shake-up, the authorities had been able to disrupt with little difficulty the attempt by reform-minded ex-communists to set up a movement with a political programme (the Socialist Movement of Czechoslovak Citizens—SMCC—which was active in 1970-72 and issued a 'Short Action Programme'). In 1972, the authorities mounted a series of ten trials of organizers of the Movement, which effectively sealed its fate. The founders of the Charter did not attempt to elaborate a political programme, but confined themselves to the statement of *fundamental* principles whose validity the government itself purportedly recognized. At the same time, the Charter capitalized on the external environment as reflected in the Final Act, and in the Czechoslovak government's ratification in 1976 of the International Covenants on Civil and Political Rights, and on Economic, Social and Cultural Rights.[12] The aim of the signatories of Charter 77 was to bring pressure on the regime to respect internationally accepted human and other rights, whose validity it had itself recognized and which had also (in 1976) been translated into Czechoslovak law. The approach could be criticized as legalistic, but by drawing the contrast between Czechoslovakia's professed commitment to detente and some of its domestic practices, the movement could hope to attract sympathy and support in the West. The emphasis on human rights, while coinciding with President Carter's championship of human rights worldwide at the opening of his presidency, was in no sense a gimmick: the Charter signatories believed the worst feature of post-1968 'normalization' lay in the denial of basic rights, for instance in job discrimination, and educational discrimination against the children of politically non-conformist parents. The Charterists' primary aim was to mobilize support at home, by initiating a dialogue with the regime, rather than to appeal to international opinion.

The emphasis on principle was also hoped to appeal to Eurocommunists in the West for whom the ideal of 'socialism with a human face' remained valid. In the event, however, Eurocommunist support has proved rather disappointing, at least as reflected in its results. The major public trial of the leading Charterists in October 1979 evoked protests from the French Communist Party amongst others, but this did not prevent the defendants from being given harsh sentences. While Eurocommunists have been openly critical of some of the repressive practices of the Czechoslovak government, they have not been ready to make a major issue of Czechoslovak 'normalization', or the treatment of Charterists, in international communist gatherings.[13] Leading members of the Czechoslovak Communist Party have, for their part, not been afraid to criticize Eurocommunists —a tendency which became especially marked after the onset of the 1980 crisis in Poland. Since 1979 there have been no further public trials of Charter or VONS members, but persecution has continued in the form of brief detentions, job discrimination and various forms of petty harassment.

The meagre results achieved by Charter 77 in its first four years stand in marked contrast to the apparent gains won by Polish workers and their advisers in 1980. This was, however, seen by most Western observers more as a reflection of Czechoslovakia's very different historical and cultural traditions than as a reason to question the tactics of the Charter. In the actual conditions, it was difficult to see what more effective methods of expressing dissent could have been found. Perhaps the most serious weakness of the Charter has lain in its apparent bias towards the interests of professional groups in preference to workers: although an increasing number of working-class signatories have been claimed (over a quarter of the total), there was little in 1980 to suggest that the movement had obtained substantial influence amongst workers. Taken as a whole, the documents published by the Charter (up to 1980) have not placed special emphasis on trade union issues, although Charter Document No. 7 on social issues (of 8 March 1977) did expressly call for free trade unions.

The most positive aspect of the Charter is that, by appealing to widely supported principles both inside and outside the country, it acts as a kind of moral conscience on the Czechoslovak leadership. In the international context, it has emphasized the adverse implications for detente of repressive and self-insulating internal policies. In the short term, such influence may have little effect; but in the medium term, the results could be more substantial. They seem most likely to be reflected not in Polish-style explosions of protest, but in the evolution of the communist party leadership. The fact that the Charter signatories include ex-communists, some of whom would welcome the chance to assist a future experiment in political reform, is relevant here.

Its stability and cohesion notwithstanding, it is possible to discern at least differences of nuance within the present Czechoslovak leadership. Two main tendencies are distinguishable, which may come to assume greater importance in the future. First, there is the tendency towards ideological dogmatism and as associated intransigence in policy-making, perhaps best typified by Vasil Bilak. Contrasting with this is a tendency towards pragmatism evidenced for instance in the down-to-earth approach of Prime Minister Strougal. Husák's own position is not easy to identify with any confidence and may perhaps best be described as that of a conservative who is none the less able to reconcile differences between the two camps. Attention has already been drawn to the uncompromising nature of Bilak's philosophy and to the difficulties in the way of its application. It amounts to a quest for almost total insulation from the pernicious influences of the West and for domestic success through the 'mobilization' of the populace by force of appeal to its ideological conscience and commitment. The pragmatists are less inflexible in their approach to the outside world and recognize that Czechoslovak socialist man cannot live by ideology alone. Although the balance has in recent years been tilting towards the dogmatists, it might go the other way if the Soviet attitude were to change and possibly also if there were changes in the external environment, for instance a new impetus to detente or if a common trend towards political liberalization were to develop in the other East European states.[14] It seems in any event probable that, when Husák eventually leaves the scene, a choice will have to be made between the opposing tendencies.

Romania

Of all the East European states, with the possible exception of Bulgaria, Romania has in recent years faced the fewest problems in managing the competing pulls of East and West, so far as their ramifications for internal stability are concerned. Romania's opening to the West has so far had only marginal effect on the domestic scene. Many Romanian intellectuals are certainly attracted by Western (especially French) values and practices (although this attraction is probably less strong than in Poland and Czechoslovakia) and voices critical of the system have occasionally been heard. However, the intelligentsia in Romania has traditionally been conformist and isolated, and it has not had the influence of its Polish and Czechoslovak counterparts. Romanian dissidents have been allowed little scope within the system. The leadership has resorted to what, in the view of the 1979 Amnesty Report on Romania, were extremely harsh measures against those who directly challenged the authority of the regime.[15] If its findings are to be believed, these measures have included internment in psychiatric hospitals and physical methods of breaking people's resistance. In parallel with this, the government has allowed not a few dissenters to emigrate. The only opposition grouping to surface in recent years, the SLOMR (Free Syndicate of Romanian Workers) was disrupted with little difficulty by the government in 1979 when the leaders were tried and given long prison sentences (some later being allowed to leave the country): there is no subsequent sign of any organized opposition. The evidence suggests that the number of dissidents, if this term is taken to connote open expression of criticism of the regime, has never been large. The signature of the Helsinki Final Act appears to have had only a small effect in stimulating forces in Romania to challenge the human rights policies of the regime.

The Romanian government has appeared to follow a policy of allowing or encouraging particularly troublesome critics to go into exile. Paul Goma, a writer and founder of a Romanian Helsinki monitoring group, was arrested in 1977 and then allowed to go into exile. Although Goma has remained an articulate critic in his present Paris abode, his ability to influence developments in his country is minimal. Meanwhile, there is no sign in Romania of the appearance of any dissident figure of comparable stature, and no more has been heard of monitoring groups.

The one recent serious domestic challenge —the Jiu Valley miners' strikes in August 1977— appears to have had entirely internal origins. The revolt, in which the Minister of Mines was for a while held by strikers, was in protest against low pay and against bad and dangerous working conditions. The ringleaders were arrested and given prison sentences. The government's tough handling of the strike did not improve its image abroad, but international press treatment was restrained and of brief duration. Internal Romanian policies have been the object of very limited interest in the Western world and have attracted less attention than Romania's independent foreign policy. The latter has undoubtedly been useful to the regime, not only promoting Romania's diplomacy, but also in distracting foreign attention from some of the less happy aspects of internal policy.

The renewal by the US Congress of Romania's MFN status in 1979 was posited on the classification of Romania as a country which permitted emigration. While it is true that Romania had been facilitating the emigration of a substantial number of ethnic Germans to the FRG under its agreement of 1967 and had been allowing fairly large numbers of Jews to emigrate, the action of the US Congress would appear to have been influenced also by its general appraisal of Romania's position in the socialist camp and its record of taking issue with the USSR. Similar considerations seem to have influenced the attitudes of other Western governments. When for example President and Madame Ceauşescu paid a state visit to France in 1979, the French authorities appear to have paid little attention to protests from Romanian émigré groups in Paris. The Romanian President's state visit to the UK in 1977 was another example of deference paid to Romania and to Ceauşescu personally, notwithstanding criticisms of the government's internal policies.

The external event which would appear to have had the greatest influence on the confidence of the Romanian leadership concerning its internal policies was the Polish crisis of 1980. Ceauşescu's first reaction was to claim that Romanian trade unions were fully responsive to the needs of Romanian workers. His government shortly afterwards took a number of steps which were apparently designed to prevent the type of protest against official privilege which was one of the features of the Polish rebellion. The Romanian parliament introduced legislation under which government and party officials were to be obliged to reveal details of their private assets. It prevented Ministers from using their privileges to acquire holiday villas. The government also scrapped plans to raise prices for food and domestic consumer products in 1981. For his part, President Ceauşescu visited Bucharest markets and also sensitive mining areas. These measures appeared to represent an admission by the party that resentment against privilege and protest against consumer scarcities could surface in Romania as well as in other bloc countries. The regime was no doubt also influenced by the fact that in the summer of 1980 there was reportedly a fresh eruption of labour unrest in Tirgoviste.

The government's plans for the economy in the 1980s, with their continuing emphasis on maintaining a high level of investment, hold the promise of very limited increments in the real earnings of Romanian workers. This may lead to some further outbreaks of unrest of the type of the Jiu Valley strikes. There is little to suggest that the regime would deal less firmly with future trouble of this kind and it is unlikely that, in such an event, much attention would be paid to such reactions as there might be in the Western media. The government may, however, be faced with a more serious problem if ordinary Romanians become increasingly influenced by developments in other bloc countries. If trade unions are given a new role in Poland, both in expressing workers' views to management and in directly influencing the formulation of government economic policy, this may lead to less compliant attitudes on the part of Romanian workers, whose official trade unions have hitherto been of the distinctly subordinate variety, typical of the democratic centralist Leninist model. The lack of any organized opposition as Romania enters the 1980s may make such a threat appear containable in the short term. But it may add to the regime's incentive to resort to repressive policies to safeguard its power. The alternative, of permitting a measure of genuine democratization, although theoretically possible, may be perceived as fraught with much more substantial risks; there is certainly little evidence in 1981 of any shift in this direction on the part of the RCP.

If, as seems likely, Romania's economic dependence on the Soviet Union increases during the 1980s, this may have some internal repercussions as well as some limiting effects on the conduct of Romanian foreign policy. But in the foreseeable future the internal effects may not be very great. So long as Ceauşescu maintains his tight grip on the RCP and is able to prevent the formation of any significant rival influence, the Soviet Union can expect to have little opportunity of influencing policy through the exploitation of men of confidence within the party (as it was able to do in Czechoslovakia in 1968). It may have as little influence in the selection of a successor to Ceauşescu as it apparently had when Ceauşescu was elected to First Secretary in 1965. However, at the beginning of the 1980s there was nothing to suggest that the Soviet Union was seriously dissatisfied with Romanian *internal* policies. While what Western observers have dubbed the 'personality cult' may not be fully to Soviet taste, this is an issue which pales in comparison with the type of problem encountered in Poland with its much more obvious and direct implications for the cohesion of the 'socialist camp'.

Why the divergence?

Of the countries surveyed, Romania is the one which has been the least affected by external influences. This is in part no doubt attributable to the lower level of Romania's economic and social development; it may also reflect the fact that, notwithstanding the identification of Romania's pre-war bourgeoisie with Western Europe and especially France, Romanian cultural and historical links with the West are more superficial than those of either Poland or Czechoslovakia. The fact that Romania has no borders with Western states and is geographically more remote than those other bloc countries is also relevant. At the same time, Romania's relative insulation has been assisted by internal policies which have promoted ideologically harmless Romanian traditions to the exclusion of less safe foreign influences in the realm of culture and education; amongst the casualties of this has been the large Hungarian minority which has suffered in terms of both cultural and educational opportunity. The maintenance of a highly centralized system of administration, with strongly endowed security services as a main pillar, has also worked towards this end. The almost daily visits to Bucharest of foreign statesmen and leaders of foreign communist parties has had little effect on the exposure of ordinary Romanians to external influence.

Since 1968, reformist and dissenting elements in Poland and Czechoslovakia have sought to promote the evolution of the political systems in which they live no longer from within the communist parties but by exerting pressure on those parties from outside. There has been a rough correspondence between the methods of Charter 77/VONS and KSS ('KOR'), the leading figures of which have had fairly frequent contact with one another. Both groups have brought moral pressure to bear on the regimes, and have been sensitive to the benefits which may be derived from detente as reflected in the Final Act, and from the sympathy of West European socialists and Eurocommunists. The strongly repressive 'administrative' solutions which the Czechoslovak authorities have favoured for the treatment of dissent have inevitably limited the freedom of manoeuvre of the Charterists and their ability to influence their compatriots. The visible practical benefits of the sympathies evoked in the West have not been great. But the principled approach of the Charter is one which could in time have an influence on the Czechoslovak leadership, while in the short term it offers a point of reference and solidarity for those who prefer a 'parallel' life to values enforced from above.

There was an obvious similarity between the original aims of KOR and VONS: both were founded to assist those unfairly treated by the authorities (KOR's original objective being confined to the defence of workers). KOR's success in expanding its influence, and in bringing pressure to bear on the authorities as evidenced in the 1978 amnesty, doubtless owed something to the less rigidly repressive approach of the Polish authorities to dissent compared with the Czechoslovak. It may also have reflected Poland's greater recent exposure to the West. However, the emergent strength of KOR in 1980 derived mainly from the combination of intense public disillusionment with economic failure and KOR's close links with Polish workers: it was the largely spontaneous actions of the latter which were the actual catalyst of change. The explanation for the very different ways in which the Polish and Czechoslovak situations have developed lies partly in the differing traditions of Polish and Czechoslovak workers. Whereas the latter have on the whole shown a disciplined and conformist approach in the face of authority, the Polish workers have developed a tradition for militant action of a kind unknown in post-war Czechoslovakia. To some extent this has reflected national traditions, and the fact that the Polish workforce includes many who have recently left the land, and are more ready to challenge authority than second- or third-generation workers. The difference also reflects the relative leniency of the Polish security services. The explanation lies additionally in the novel phenomenon whereby, since 1976, Polish workers (particularly activists in Gdansk and the towns of the Baltic seaboard) and Polish intellectuals have co-operated in recognition of a community of interest. Such co-operation had not, by mid-1981, developed in any other bloc state.

In sum, it may be concluded that, in the period since 1970, internal factors were of somewhat greater importance than external factors in stimulating internal change in all the countries surveyed. Tough 'administrative' methods of dealing with the regimes' critics helped to account for the relative weakness of dissidents and opposition in Czechoslovakia and Romania. External factors were, however, a highly significant component in the Polish developments which culminated in the crisis of 1980/81, principally in the form of the encouragement which critical elements in society derived from detente and the Final Act. The Pope's visit had a strong impact, particularly in illuminating the limitations of the power exercised by the party. Also important was the Gierek regime's interest in maintaining good relations with the West and, as a corollary of this, its interest in retaining a 'liberal' image so far as domestic policy was concerned. In Czechoslovakia, the appeal of Western values, which found strong expression in the Prague spring and, later, necessarily muted expression in Charter 77, presents a medium-term challenge to the present style of leadership. In Romania, Western influence has so far had little overt impact on the internal scene, though the 1980/81 developments in Poland have suggested that the regime may feel vulnerable to the expression of discontent by Romanian workers.

7 Czechoslovakia 1968; Poland 1980: the international dimension

By a curious coincidence, the major crises in Eastern Europe have occurred at twelve-year intervals: 1956, 1968, 1980. During 1968 the Czechoslovak leaders were acutely conscious of the Soviet intervention in Hungary in 1956 but drew incomplete lessons from this. In 1980 the Poles were similarly conscious of the 1968 experience of Czechoslovakia. At the time of writing it is not possible to attempt a precise comparison since the Polish crisis is not yet over and indeed the immense problems faced by Poland, both political and economic, may take years to resolve. There are, however, interesting parallels and differences between the reactions of the Soviet Union and of other Pact countries to the events of the Prague spring and summer, and the events of the Polish summer and autumn 1980.

Origins of the crises

Perhaps the most striking difference between the two crises in the internal realm was that whereas in Czechoslovakia in 1968 the impetus for change came largely from within the communist party itself, in Poland in 1980 it was forces in society outside the party which were the catalyst of change. In Poland the demand for change, as has been seen, originated with Polish workers whose organization of strikes was largely spontaneous, although as the crisis deepened during the summer they were offered increasing assistance from KOR, from Catholic intellectuals and from circles close to the Cardinal. Their actions provoked far-reaching changes in the communist party involving the resignation of Gierek and the emergence of Kania as the new First Secretary. The strikes in the summer of 1980 were, however, only one aspect of a wider malaise which was felt within as well as outside the Polish Communist Party. The bankruptcy of the economic policies of the Gierek team, the widespread evidence of corruption, and the manifest failure of a discredited leadership to win popular backing, had already been recognized for some time by undogmatic members of the Polish United Workers' Party such as Rakowski, the editor of *Polityka*. Rakowski and like-minded pragmatists in the party acknowledged the malaise in society and the urgent need for reforms to rectify this.[1] Although the scale of the disruption to the economy occasioned by the strikes was regretted by reform-minded communists, they derived at least some gratification from the fact that the party had been forced radically to review its policies. As in Czechoslovakia in 1968, there was a certain coalescence of interest between communist reformers and non-communist elements in society. However, the differences in the two situations are more marked than the parallels. Whereas reformers were in clear ascendancy in the Czechoslovak Communist Party after January 1968, in Poland in 1980 the top echelons of the PUWP remained in the hands of men whose natural preference was for authoritarian methods of government and whose proclaimed interest in limited reforms, for instance of the economy, appeared to be more a response to overwhelming pressures from society than to inner conviction. Rakowski's belief that radical changes were required, including greater participation from below, in the formulation of party policies, while not uncommon at lower levels of the party, appeared to be shared by few in the Politburo itself.[2] It must also be noted that Rakowski's own conversion to the cause of renewal came somewhat late in the day to be wholly convincing.

The issue of control

Viewed from a Soviet perspective, the maintenance of the leading role of the communist party was in both crises an issue of crucial importance. This was not only because of Soviet fears that the erosion of party control could provide an opening for counter-revolution leading to secession from the bloc; it was also because the Soviet Union's ability to influence policy, for instance in the realm of security and foreign affairs, depended directly on the degree of control exercised by a bloc communist party. In Czechoslovakia in 1968 the question of control was an issue on which there was a remarkable failure of communication between the Soviet and Czechoslovak leaderships. Dubček and most of his entourage remained convinced, up to the point of the invasion in August, that they were fully in control. This control was in Soviet eyes being gradually and steadily eroded with non-communist elements playing an increasingly large part in developments. While it can be argued that the Soviet view of developments was exaggerated, it was indisputable that the initiatives for reform taken by innovators in the Czechoslovak Communist Party unleashed forces in society which had the effect both of reinforcing reformist tendencies in the communist party and of making it more difficult for the communist party fully to control the pace of change: far-reaching institutional changes were being promoted by increasingly vocal elements outside the party. The 'Two Thousand Words' manifesto and the formation of non-party clubs such as KAN and K231 were examples of the way in which initiative passed outside the party. Dubček and other party leaders rationalized this situation by claiming that the policies they were pursuing enjoyed the widest possible support. But in the eyes of the Soviet leaders, and of Gomulka and Ulbricht, the fact that non-communist forces in society were increasingly able to exert influence represented a serious threat to the communist party's ability to maintain control. This was also the view of the conservatives inside the Czechoslovak Communist Party. The difference in perception is aptly illustrated in the story relayed by R. Selucky of an exchange between Brezhnev and Dubček. When Brezhnev questioned whether the Czechoslovak leaders were properly controlling events, Dubček pointed to the evidence of massive support for his reform course in a petition of endorsement signed by four million Czechs and Slovaks. Brezhnev, on the contrary, saw the petition, which was of spontaneous origin, as yet a further sign of the Czechoslovak party's inability to assert control from above.[3]

The feature of the Prague spring which is likely to have most alarmed the Soviet Union was the perceived threat to the principle of democratic centralism. One aspect of this was the preparedness of leading Czechoslovak reformers to allow a degree of political pluralism, for instance in permitting the hitherto dummy parties in the National Unity Front to make a genuinely independent contribution, and in encouraging the Czechoslovak parliament to voice criticisms instead of merely acting as a rubber-stamping agency. Another aspect was the reformists' acceptance of the concept of factionalism within the communist party itself: in marked contrast to Soviet practice, it was anticipated that minorities within the party might defend their viewpoint publicly even after a contrary decision had been adopted by majority vote. Poland in 1980 exhibited some of the same tendencies. There were for example indications that the Democratic and Peasant parties in the National Unity Front were to be allowed to play an active and somewhat more assertive part on the political stage, albeit still within the confines of acceptance of the PUWP's leading role. More worrying, the successes of independent trade unions' confrontation with the regime and the apparent acceptance by the regime of unions which in principle could remain free of party control appeared to open up the prospect of a permanent non-party force in society, with its own source of legitimacy, which might in practice act as an organized and institutionalized check on the party, notwithstanding the unions' formal acknowledgement of the leading role of the PUWP. (While, of course, other constraints on the regime have existed in Poland for a long time, these have not been of an institutionalized nature.) The close association of KOR and Catholic intellectual groups with the workers' cause could be seen as the harbinger of future co-operation between unions and dissident intellectuals which would challenge the communist party's monopoly of power. Viewed from the vantage-point of the PUWP it was clearly desirable to circumscribe as far as possible the scope for overtly political action by Solidarity. An option which at the turn of the year remained open was that of taking prophylactic action against KOR and other dissident groups with a view to preventing the further strengthening of their influence with the unions (although in the summer of 1980 the new unions had made the liberation of arrested KOR members one of the conditions of their settlement with the government).

The forces at play in Czechoslovakia in 1968 have been described by the author of the most detailed work on the Czechoslovak crisis[4] as 'revolutionary': in his view, a situation had been reached in which it was no longer possible for the rulers to govern in the old way. There was a breakdown of the established order which fitted Lenin's classic formula. The changes involved the gradual loss of power by the party bureaucracy and a dramatic shift of forces within the party and within society as a whole. All social groups, with the partial exception of the peasants, were drawn into the crisis. A revolutionary situation is one which by definition is difficult to control and Dubček was very far from being in the mould of a Robespierre or a Lenin. Poland in 1980 displayed some similar features: the credibility of the ruling elite had been so far diminished that it felt constrained to make major concessions to non-party forces. The PUWP list the initiative, and its new-found commitment to reform was the direct result of pressures from society. However, the circumstances of the unleashing of social forces varied considerably in the two instances. In Poland the communist party had become increasingly demoralized in the latter half of the 1970s and its will to introduce unpopular economic remedies was paralysed after the workers' protest of 1976. The party had virtually lost the ability to govern so far as the formulation of constructive economic policy was concerned. Although in 1977-80 pragmatists in the party were acquiring rather greater influence, the economic problems were so severe and public disillusionment so intense that the existing leadership confronted a gargantuan task in any attempt it might make to mobilize public opinion behind new policies. The party's immobility was finally shaken by the rash of strikes in the summer of 1980.

In Czechoslovakia the communist reformers did not confront an economic crisis as such. Czechoslovak reformers believed, it is true, that the perpetuation of highly centralist economic policies had denied the country opportunities to achieve more efficient and faster growth. However, discontent in Czechoslovak society derived more from a widespread general feeling of dissatisfaction with an ossified political and economic system which had been slow to shed its Stalinist features than with specific economic grievances. Unlike the Poles in 1979-80, the Czechoslovaks in 1968 had not just experienced a severe drop in their living standards coupled with growing shortages of basic goods, and significantly there was no serious labour unrest in Czechoslovakia. The impulse for reform was generated not by workers but by intellectuals who cheekily proclaimed that they had discovered a better model for Czechoslovak development than that bequeathed by Moscow. In sum, the Polish communists found themselves fighting a desperate battle to restore public confidence after Polish workers had protested violently against the results of manifestly bankrupt economic policies. The Czechoslovak communists in 1968 launched what they perceived as an ambitious new model of socialism in the belief that the relatively advanced state of Czechoslovak economic development, coupled with the country's cultural traditions and Western democratic affinities, justified a departure from Soviet norms. The Action Programme drawn up by the reform communists had the effect of stimulating non-communist forces in society to emerge from their isolation; but the Programme itself was not primarily a response to these forces.

Censorship

During the Prague spring and summer, the lifting of censorship gave cause for much concern both in the Soviet Union and to its more hardline allies. In their new-found freedom the Czechoslovak news media not only challenged the conventional wisdom about the nature of the Czechoslovak political system but also engaged in direct criticism of the Soviet Union and its allies. The new-found licence of the Czechoslovak media was unquestionably one of the main factors which influenced the Soviet decision to intervene. In Poland in 1980/81 the more liberal approach to censorship carried similar risks of provocation. However, Polish editors showed considerable awareness of the damage which might ensue from any display of 'anti-Sovietism'. The control exercised by the PUWP over the media, especially TV, was distinctly tighter than had been the case in Czechoslovakia in 1968. Criticism of internal failure was relatively frank and there was an increasing tendency during the second half of 1980 to give coverage to dissenting viewpoints, including the positions taken by Solidarity. But criticism of the Soviet Union and

Poland's Warsaw Pact allies was eschewed. The Polish authorities paid particular attention to this aspect in the drafting of new legislation on censorship which was due to be brought before the Sejm at the end of 1980. It was expected that the legislation would require the media to avoid comment which challenged Poland's alliances and the basic foundations of its political system, including the leading role of the communist party.

Ideology and the Czech variant

A further major difference between the two crises lay in the contrast between the-self-confidence of the 1968 Czech and Slovak reformers in their claim to be enunciating a new model of communism, and the confused and groping response to events of the Polish communists in 1980. The Czech and Slovak reformers took ideology seriously and reached the conclusion that a radically different model of communism from that developed in Moscow was required for an economically and culturally advanced country such as Czechoslovakia. Although they made no claims for its suitability elsewhere in the bloc, it was hardly surprising that conservatives in the Soviet Union and in other bloc states viewed the attempt with considerable apprehension. It was feared that the Prague experiment could have destabilizing effects which might even threaten the cohesion of the Soviet Union itself: an example of this was the acute anxiety expressed by Shelest, the Ukrainian party leader, who took an even more alarmist view than the Polish and East German leaders.

In Poland, the bulk of reformers within the PUWP staked out rather less ambitious claims (though there were exceptions). The emphasis was on the need to develop new methods of party operation which would offer guarantees against the corruption and abuse of power which had characterized the 1970s, rather than on the need for ideological revision. Talk about the need for 'renewal' was not accompanied by calls for an actual 'new model' of socialism. There was no direct challenge to the authority of the Soviet Union. The grass-roots pressures in the PUWP for horizontal structures, which gained strength in the early part of 1981, did however contain the seeds of revisionism. The election by secret ballot of candidates for the Central Committee (in July 1981) could also be interpreted as a challenge to hitherto accepted practice within the bloc. Mounting Soviet concern was reflected in the communiqué issued at the end of the Twenty-sixth Party Congress in Moscow which expressed Soviet confidence in the Polish leaders' ability to 'reverse the course of events' and two months later (in April 1981) when Pravda declaimed against the dangers of 'revisionism' in Poland. None the less, there was (up to the time when this book goes to press) little or no sign in Poland of a number of the heresies which sprang up during the Prague spring. Leading Polish communist reformers did not suggest that opposition be institutionalized (except insofar as their tolerance of Solidarity could be taken to imply acceptance of some degree of check on state power). Nor did Polish reformers repeat the Prague reformers' attempt (in the KSC draft statutes published in the summer of 1968) to allow a minority in the party the right to express a dissenting opinion after a majority position had been established. This challenge to one of the central tenets of 'democratic centralism' was arguably more serious than the free balloting at the 1981 Party Congress in Poland.

The Soviet Union later developed the theory that Czechoslovakia was subject to a 'quiet counter-revolution' the end result of which would have been, but for the fact of intervention, the complete overthrow of socialism. In the Soviet interpretation, the Czechoslovak party was being gradually infiltrated by elements working towards that end. In Poland, the Soviet leadership initially took the rather different view that the Polish communists, while guilty of mismanagement of the economy, of laxity in permitting corruption in party ranks to spread, and of political ineptitude in their failure to retain credibility, were threatened not with counter-revolution from within their ranks but with the risk of subversion from without if they failed to restore a degree of confidence. When Gierek resigned, the new leadership took care to consult Moscow and sought its active support: Stanislaw Kania's own trip to Moscow in October 1980 was undertaken apparently at his own initiative and was evidently designed not only to solicit economic assistance but also to win understanding for the Polish regime's efforts to restore confidence through a mixture of firm measures to reassert the party's control, limited reforms and a degree of co-operation with the independent Solidarity union. Reliable sources in Moscow in December 1980 were quoted as saying that Kania had been given the clear message in October that he would obtain and could rely upon Soviet backing, provided that he maintained Poland's alliances and strengthened the leading role of the communist party.[6]

In the run-up to the Polish Party Congress in the spring of 1981, the Soviet attitude grew less benevolent. As already noted, the charge was made that 'revisionist' influences were at work within the PUWP. However, the Soviet leadership did not go so far as to question the intentions of the Kania leadership: it was the efficacy of the methods employed to achieve them which were called in question.

Military/security risks

Another serious source of anxiety in the 1968 Czechoslovak crisis was the possible repercussions on the military strength of the Warsaw Treaty alliance. The Soviet Union was alarmed by the fact that after the dismissal of the reformist General Prchlik, who had publicly criticized the way in which the Soviet Union treated its junior partners in the Warsaw Pact, the department of the Czechoslovak Communist Party which supervised the military and police was abolished. Control passed in effect from the party to the government. There were also indications that the concern of the Soviet military was heightened by reports of the stationing by NATO countries of substantial forces along all the borders of Warsaw Pact countries including Czechoslovakia. The issue of control over the military and security forces did not arise in the Polish 1980 crisis. Kania's own role in the PUWP before taking on the First Secretaryship had been to exercise control over the armed forces and the police, and the Kremlin can have had little reason to fear that he would be ready to sacrifice party control in this vital area. The appointment of General Jaruzelski as Prime Minister in early 1981 provided added reassurance in this sphere. The two Soviet armoured divisions in Poland were not exposed to any immediate threats. The Soviet press did however show sensitivity to the possible risk to the security of supply lines to East Germany if instability in Poland were to increase further. When Polish railway workers took strike action in November, the Soviet media pointed to the imperative need to preserve the Warsaw Pact's defensive strength (even though the Polish strikers made clear their intention was not to jeopardize the supply lines).

The external environment

Although at first sight the external environment in 1980 was very different from that in 1968, there were some similarities as well as differences. In 1968 the Soviet Union was showing interest in detente but was unsure about the attitude of the FRG and the United States, and was concerned to strengthen its negotiating position before engaging in substantive talks. It was extremely nervous that independent moves by East European allies, such as the establishment of diplomatic relations between Romania and the FRG in January 1967, might undermine the basis for a concerted negotiation with the West of the outstanding issues of security and co-operation in Europe (as later materialized in the CSCE talks of the early 1970s). In 1980, the Soviet Union could look back on a number of successes in the conduct of its foreign policy, the most important of which was the confirmation of the European territorial and political status quo in the Helsinki Final Act. Successes had also been achieved in strengthening the cohesion of the socialist camp, for instance through the reforms of the Warsaw Pact of 1969 and the elaboration of the Comprehensive Programme of Integration in 1969-71. The Kremlin was less preoccupied at the opening of the 1980s with the problems of consolidating its hold over Eastern Europe than it had been in 1968. Although Romania continued to display independence in the conduct of its foreign policy and in occasionally challenging Soviet policies in bloc institutions, the degree of defiance was not noticeably greater in 1980 than it had been twelve years before; there were indeed signs that the potential challenge to the USSR had diminished, given the shift in the Romanian attitude towards Comecon (see Chapters 2 and 6), and the greater Romanian economic reliance on the Soviet Union evidenced for example in the importation for the first time (in 1980) of Soviet oil. Ceauşescu's evident misgivings about the course of events in Poland will have strengthened his perception of the benefits of the Soviet connection. At the May 1980 meeting of the Warsaw Pact Political Consultative Committee (on the occasion of the twenty-fifth anniversary of the founding of the Warsaw Pact), the Pact countries were able to demonstrate a considerable degree of bloc unity in the wake of the NATO decision (December 1979) to modernize its theatre nuclear forces by placing land-based nuclear missiles in Western Europe. While the Soviet invasion of Afghanistan had been greeted by some bloc governments (most notably the Romanian, but also the Polish and Hungarian) with less than total enthusiasm, the partial disagreement on this issue did not seriously threaten bloc unity. The Afghanistan affair illustrated the way in which Poland, Hungary and Romania had acquired a greater stake in detente than their bloc partners, but this did not prevent the Pact from presenting a common front at the Madrid CSCE Review Meeting in November 1980.

Both the Czechoslovak reform leaders in 1968 and the Polish communists in 1980 laid great stress on their respective countries' alliances with the Soviet Union. Despite this superficial similarity, however, there was a certain difference in motivation. The Czechoslovak reformers were hoping to persuade the Kremlin, by avoiding Imre Nagy's fatal mistake of abandoning the Warsaw Pact and of effectively abandoning the leading role of the party, and by affirming their dedication to the alliance with the Soviet Union, that reform did not threaten the cohesion of the socialist camp. The Polish leaders, while also anxious to give proof of their loyalty to the Soviet Union, were preoccupied above all with their need to prevent the spontaneous movement of protest, sparked off by the strikes, from either assuming an anti-Soviet direction or from exceeding the threshold of Soviet tolerance. The argument was employed that the communist party bore a special responsibility for the development of detente in Europe. In a speech in Gdansk, the Politburo member with responsibility for the economy, Stefan Olszowski, emphasized the importance of Poland for 'the stability of the international situation' and declared that Poles 'must not allow a weakening of our position in the world, both among friends and towards Western countries'.[7] Thus it was being suggested that moderation and continued loyalty to the Soviet Union were essential conditions for maintaining a foreign policy which could safeguard the special benefits for Poland of detente. The theme that internal stabilization in Poland was a matter of considerable international consequence was not confined to apologists of government policy. Rakowski, in *Polityka*, also took the line that Poland's special international position demanded that confrontation between government and unions be replaced by co-operation. Ironically, in an interview with members of Solidarity published in *Polityka*, the journal's staff even attempted to convince trade unionists of the virtues of moderation by quoting counsels for restraint in the foreign press including a reference in *Le Figaro* to 'irresponsible claims' which went beyond 'the country's present limited possibilities'.[8]

There were some very different nuances in the approach of Czechoslovak reformers in 1968 and that of Polish communists in 1980 in terms of the pursuit of national goals in foreign policy. Although in 1968 the Czechoslovak reform leadership did not (as described in Chapter 4) take foreign policy initiatives which caused the Soviet Union any embarrassment, the references in the Action Programme to the need for a 'more active' foreign policy and for more specifically Czechoslovak initiatives, for instance in the United Nations, were probably viewed with a degree of anxiety in the Kremlin: the reformers certainly appeared to be ready to interpret the obligations of alliance in a somewhat more elastic way than their predecessors. The new Kania government in Poland, on the other hand, gave no sign of wishing to experiment in the sphere of foreign policy; it was indeed hardly in a position of sufficient strength to do so. The emphasis was rather on the necessity of maintaining the closest co-operation with the USSR precisely to serve Polish goals. Looked at from a Soviet perspective, this is likely to be found distinctly more reassuring than the parroted Czechoslovak reaffirmations of bloc loyalties during the summer of 1968.

Perhaps the most striking external parallel between 1968 and 1980 was in the anxiety aroused by the destabilization of a bloc state amongst its East European neighbours. In the Czechoslovak case it was of course the German Democratic Republic and Poland who evinced the greatest anxiety. The GDR authorities were partly concerned about the risks of political and ideological contamination. For this reason they banned the importation into the GDR of German-language journals published in Prague. Another particular worry for the GDR derived from the relatively relaxed policies of the Dubček leadership with regard to Czechoslovak frontiers: restrictions on obtaining entry visas to Czechoslovakia were virtually lifted and they were reports that some of the electric and barbed-wire fences with Austria had been removed. The GDR, which had gone to such trouble and had incurred much international opprobrium in sealing off its own western borders, did not relish the opening of a new uncontrolled exit route; its response was to create barbed-wire fences on the border with Czechoslovakia and to refuse (along with the USSR) tourist visas to visit Czechoslovakia.

The Polish crisis of 1980 also gave rise to concern in the GDR about its borders. In October 1980, East Berlin suspended the arrangements agreed in 1972 whereby Poles and East Germans could visit each other's respective countries without visas. For its part, the Husák regime in Czechoslovakia made it more difficult (by insisting on production of letters of invitation) for Poles to visit Czechoslovakia as tourists, and for Czechs and Slovaks to visit Poland, and introduced currency restrictions. The parallel between 1968 and 1980 is, however, not an exact one so far as border restrictions are concerned. One of the main worries of Czechoslovakia's neighbours in 1968 was that the country would be used as an escape route to the West.[9] In 1980/81 the principal fear of both the East German and the Czechoslovak authorities appears to have been the contamination of their citizens through exposure to political turbulence in neighbouring Poland. At the same time, these authorities were no doubt anxious to reduce to a minimum the possibilities for contacts to be developed between dissidents in their countries and 'anti-socialist forces' in Poland. A subsidiary motive, in the case of the GDR, was to prevent increasing numbers of Poles in the border areas from crossing to the GDR in order to buy up the many commodities that were in such short supply in Poland.

In both crises the hardline neighbours of the countries in crisis were worried above all by the risks which deviation from traditional orthodoxy might pose for the stability of their own regimes: in this sense Honecker and Husák in 1980 could be described as almost exact counterparts to Ulbricht and Gomulka in 1968. East German and Czechoslovak press comment on developments in Poland was often sharply critical, as also were statements by leading members of the two bloc communist parties. The most threatening message was delivered by Honecker himself, who said that the aim of opposition forces in Poland was 'not to make socialism more human, but to eliminate it'. He declared that Poland was, and would remain, a socialist country and that 'we, together with our friends, will make sure of this'. He also took the occasion to revive memories of 1968 by roundly attacking the FRG for policies of 'gaining military preponderance and interference on a worldwide scale', in the affairs of others.[10] In Czechoslovakia, V. Bilak is reported to have told the Czechoslovak Central Committee that the allegedly non-political promoters of independent unions in Poland aimed to turn these 'into a legal base for opposition activity and a main channel for interference in the Polish People's Republic from abroad.[11] The Czechoslovak and East German press carried only emasculated and distorted accounts of the successes of Solidarity. Their line, which was similar in most respects to that of the Soviet media—but often more emotionally charged — contrasted with the relatively open coverage of events in Poland given by the Hungarian press.

The coverage of events in Poland in the Czechoslovak media may in fact have at least partly reflected inter-factional conflicts between hard-liners and pragmatists in the Czechoslovak leadership. There were some signs that the Bilak line was not entirely shared by Strougal and even Husák (for instance, reports of what was said to Kádár when he met Husák in late November). In December, Herr Genscher was reportedly given to understand, during an official visit to Prague, that his inter-locutors wished for less attention to be paid, and less drama attached, to Polish developments.

Possibly the least predictable reaction in 1980 was that of Romania. As in 1968 during the Czechoslovak crisis, President Ceauşescu laid formal stress on the preservation of national sovereignty and on the need scrupulously to observe the principle of non-interference in the internal affairs of other states: it was for the Polish Communist Party and people to resolve their own difficulties. However, he coupled this (perhaps not altogether consistently) with direct criticism of the performance of the Polish leadership in managing the economy and in failing to adopt 'decisive attitudes towards anti-socialist forces'. He also criticized the persistence in Poland of non-socialist forms of production: 'there is no doubt that as long as economic sectors based on different foundations exist, the class struggle will endure and re-emerge in one or another form'. He went on to question the ideological basis for 'indepen-dent trade unions', asking 'independent from whom?'[12] Ceauşescu's anxieties in 1980 appeared in fact to be of a rather different complexion from those of 1968: while in the latter year he was worried above all by the threat of Soviet interference in the sovereign affairs of a bloc state, in 1980 he appeared more anxious about the threat which independent unions posed to the Polish Communist Party's ability to sustain its monopoly of power.

The explanation for this Romanian shift of attitude is no doubt partly to be found in the fact that while in 1968 the central issue appeared to be the ability of the leadership of a bloc country to go its own way, accepting minimal guidance from the Soviet Union in the formulation of internal policies, the threat in Poland came not from within the Polish leadership but from forces which appeared to put at risk the whole structure of power. It is of course arguable that the Dubček experiment could, had it not been aborted by Soviet intervention, have led to a similar challenge to communist control. If however Ceauşescu perceived such a risk in 1968, he was clearly disposed to accord it a lower priority than what he perceived to be the threat to national sovereignty. In 1980, sovereignty was not the immediate issue: there was no evidence of any conflict between the Soviet and Polish leaderships which could be compared to the dispute which developed between the Dubcek team and the Soviet leaders in March—August 1968. Ceauşescu's changed emphasis in 1980 may well also have reflected his awareness that Romania herself was vulnerable to popular discontent in reaction to economic policies which failed to raise living standards. While Romania had been registering markedly higher growth rates than Poland in the second half of the 1970s, the growth in real disposable incomes was less impressive. Romanian living standards remained distinctly the lowest in the bloc. The Jiu Valley strikes of 1977 had shown that working-class discontent might erupt at any time, and there were reports in the summer of 1980 of renewed industrial unrest in the mining and other areas.[13]

In the Soviet Union itself, official reaction to Polish events was slightly more measured than that of the Czechoslovak and GDR media, though there were clear enough indications that the Kremlin shared some of the anxieties of the hardline states. The Soviet press intimated that the old unions were being victimized, and reminded their readers of the Leninist principle that unions must carry out party policy. A particularly ominous warning was delivered in early December when Solidarity officials were accused of initiating a campaign to replace trade union officials with people who were 'openly acting from anti-government positions' and 'leading the country to further destabilization and aggravation of the political struggle'.[14] The report also alleged that factory guards had been disarmed by Solidarity members. The Western press pointed to parallels with 1968, for instance the Soviet press reports prior to the invasion that arms caches had been found in Western Bohemia. But the Soviet press dropped the story quickly after the Polish authorities denied its veracity, and there was no follow-up.

At the end of November, the Soviet media reprinted a strong Czechoslovak attack on Polish developments, drawing clear parallels between 1968 and 1980. This included the Brezhnev Doctrine-type formulations that the 'indomitable strength' of socialism lay in its 'internationalist solidarity'.[15] However, the Soviet media on no occasion accused Polish communists of entertaining revisionist notions; they did not directly call in doubt the Polish party's concessions to the new trade unions, and did not try to present these as a threat to ideological orthodoxy (as, by implication, did some of the GDR and Czechoslovak comment). In this respect there was a clear distinction between the Soviet attitude in the Polish and Czechoslovak crises: in the latter, the Soviet complaint had been very much with the policies of the Czech party itself.

In early December, Western media carried reports based mainly on US intelligence to the effect that the Soviet Union had brought its military units on Poland's borders to a strength and state of readiness which would have been consistent with a plan to intervene in Poland.

There is no direct evidence of actual Soviet intentions at this time. Some plausibility may be attached to Yugoslav suggestions that the moves were 'stage thunder' designed to demonstrate to Poles the gravity of the situation and the consequent need for moderation of union demands. Shortly afterwards, at any rate, Soviet spokesmen went out of their way to emphasize that they looked to Poland to resolve its own difficulties, and that there was no question of planned Soviet interference.[16] It may have been no coincidence that the demonstration of Soviet military strength came shortly after Solidarity had challenged the Polish security services by circulating a filched secret instruction regarding means of tackling dissidents. If it was in fact the Soviet intention to stage a show of strength in order to prevent hotheads in Solidarity from going over the brink, some success could have been claimed: it was at this point that Walesa declared that 'we are all Poles first, members of Solidarity second'. Shortly afterwards, the Primate counselled restraint in an important sermon.

Western responses

The attitude of Western governments with regard to Poland during the summer and autumn of 1980 bore some early resemblances to those displayed in 1968 during the run-up to Soviet intervention in Czechoslovakia, but as the Polish crisis developed some different nuances appeared. The governments of NATO member states showed considerable restraint in the early months of the Polish crisis. They adopted the position that it should be left to Poles to sort out their troubles without outside interference. Although the country against which the latter injunction was mainly directed was not hard to guess, Western governments eschewed provocative statements. While President Carter, in his election campaign, could not resist claiming the Gdansk Agreement between the Polish government and the Inter-Factory Committee as a 'victory for human rights', his main message was one of gratification that the crisis had apparently been resolved by 'peaceful determination'. When Lord Carrington visited Poland in October, he was careful to avoid comment on Polish internal developments. In November the NATO Secretary General, Joseph Luns, stated in unambiguous terms that NATO countries were not contemplating military action in response to events in Poland.

The restraint of Western governments did not prevent Warsaw Pact countries from denouncing what was described in the communiqué issued at the end of Kania's visit to Moscow on 20 October 1980 as attempted 'subversion' by 'certain imperialist circles'.[17] Soviet, Czechoslovak and East German commentators were quick to denounce such things as the reported dispatch of financial support by Western trade unions to assist the newly formed Polish unions.[18] There were also reports alleging that Radio Free Europe was sending coded messages to opposition groups in Poland. However, while it was alleged that anti-communist circles in the West were waging a psychological war against Poland and other communist countries, the criticisms in nearly all cases only indirectly impugned Western governments. (The attacks by the GDR on the FRG at the early stage of the crisis were in no sense typical, and may have been designed primarily as a warning that intra-German relations would suffer if Bonn attempted any form of interference; possibly also it was hoped thereby to isolate the East German population from the FRG.) The most overt instance of complaints being made against the policies of governments as opposed to organizations was in October 1980, when the US, FRG and UK ambassadors were reportedly summoned to the Polish Foreign Ministry to be warned of Polish displeasure at the activities of Western news media. During the 1968 Czech crisis, attacks by Eastern media on Western governments were more direct, with particular attention being directed to the allegedly nefarious intentions of the FRG.

Western governments adopted a higher profile following the news reports in early December 1980 that the Soviet Union was bringing its units on Polish borders to a higher state of readiness, and was conducting manoeuvres. These reports were reflected in a robust NATO statement on the occasion of the semi-annual ministerial meeting in December. The NATO Ministers made it clear that Soviet intervention in Poland was likely to have grave consequences for detente. It was announced that NATO ambassadors had been instructed to draw up a contingency plan spelling out the details of possible responses to a Soviet move against Poland. It was intimated that these were likely to include economic sanctions.[19] The attitude thus adopted was in some respects imprecise (for instance, it was not made clear what type and degree of economic sanctions might be adopted). But nevertheless it stood in marked contrast to the low profile adopted by Western countries in the run-up to the Soviet invasion of Czechoslovakia in 1968 when President Brezhnev had been able to claim (according to Mlynar's account) that he had been given an assurance by President Johnson that the United States would take no action in the event of intervention.

There are three other differences in Western attitudes to the two crises which are worth noting. The first is that the Polish crisis attracted wider and more sustained public interest than did the unfolding of the Czechoslovak crisis, if the actual military intervention in Czechoslovakia and the two months immediately preceding it are excluded. In 1980, Western imagination was captured by the fact that the working class in a major communist country was overtly defying a communist party whose *raison d'être* was to defend workers' interests. The revelations about the incompetence and corruption of disgraced former members of the Polish leadership and bureaucracy testified to the profundity of the country's moral crisis, while the gravity of Poland's economic problems was a matter of both political and economic concern to the West. In Czechoslovakia in 1968 it was possible, up till the moment of invasion, to dismiss the reform debate as an argument primarily between rival groups within a communist party whose dedication to Marxism and allegiance to the Warsaw Pact were not in question. The pressures exerted by the Soviet Union and other Warsaw Pact states could be interpreted as being an attempt to influence that debate in the direction of ideological orthodoxy. The actual debate, while of considerable interest to Western communist parties and to Western specialists in communist affairs, was of less interest to broad groups in Western society than was the confrontation between government and workers and other groups in society which developed in Poland in the second half of 1980. This was a confrontation not between rival sects of Marxist–Leninists but between a badly tarnished communist party and non-communist groups who hoped to establish permanent checks on the abuse of power. The existence of large Polish communities in a number of Western countries, most notably the United States (with an estimated population of Polish descent of twelve million), also helped to stimulate interest: the fact that President Carter's Secretary of State and his National Security Council Adviser were both of Polish extraction was but one reminder of the way in which Polish–American links were likely to feature largely in the event of a threat to Poland's sovereignty.

The second difference lay in the fact that, whereas Western economic interest in Czechoslovakia in 1968 was of negligible proportions, the scale of Poland's trade with the West and, still more importantly, of its indebtedness, made the Polish crisis of direct concern to Western bankers and businessmen as well as to governments. The fact that Western governments responded in most cases sympathetically to Polish requests for new assistance no doubt helped to reassure the Polish authorities and the Kremlin that Western statesmen were not attempting to 'destabilize' the situation further, or otherwise exploit the crisis. Arguably, the size of the Western stake in Poland had the effect of making Western governments show still greater restraint than could otherwise have been expected.

The third difference derived from the fact of the signature in 1975 of the Helsinki Final Act, in which all signatories had pledged to respect *inter alia* the principle of non-intervention in the internal affairs of other signatory states (Principle VI in the Declaration of Principles). The effect of this was twofold. In the first place, the Final Act clearly established a link between detente and respect for sovereignty and autonomy. Although the December 1979 invasion of Afghanistan had suggested that Soviet respect for this principle outside Europe was, to put it at its lowest, open to question, the Soviet leaders can have been in little doubt that its breach in a country at the centre of Europe would have jeopardized detente and with it most of the benefits the USSR continued to derive from the Final Act. The second factor was the much heightened awareness in the West of the link between détente and respect for human rights. President Carter in 1977 had made this a main plank of his foreign policy. A suppression of the assertion of basic rights in Poland would have represented a clear defeat for those who pinned hopes on the human rights provisions of the Final Act.

The robust stance on Poland adopted by NATO in December 1980 reflected amongst other things a realization by the West European countries with the greatest stake in détente – most notably the FRG and France – that armed Soviet intervention would cause the collapse of détente in Europe. There was also an awareness in the West that even interference in Polish affairs which stopped short of armed intervention would have serious consequences for detente if the result were the suppression of the forces which had been seeking to assert basic rights (such as the right to organize unions genuinely representative of workers' views).[20]

Although this is unlikely to have been one of the Kremlin's most pressing preoccupations, the stance adopted by Western communist parties was more widely and strongly sympathetic to liberalizing currents over Poland in 1980 than over the Prague spring. It is true that the Italian Communist Party in 1968 showed clear sympathy for the Dubček experiment; this together with the sympathetic attitude adopted by the Yugoslav and Romanian ruling parties, provided moral even if little practical support for the Czech and Slovak reformers. In 1980 the majority of Western European communist parties, as well as the Yugoslav (though, as seen, not the Romanian) showed sympathy for the cause of reform. The only major exception was the French Communist Party, which was reluctant to acknowledge the gravity of the Polish crisis and showed little enthusiasm for the cause of the independent unions; while it never displayed the uncompromising hostility to that cause of the East German and Czechoslovak leaders, its acceptance of milestones towards reform such as the Gdansk Agreement was at best grudging and ambivalent. Other Western communist parties however, including the British, were quick to recognize that, without fundamental reforms, the communist system in Poland faced moral bankruptcy. The activities of Solidarity were seen as a necessary ingredient in an inevitable process of change.[21]

Main parallels and contrasts

The main similarity between the two crises was that in each there was—at least in Soviet eyes—a threat to the ability of a bloc communist party to maintain control and to preserve ideological orthodoxy. The two dangers were of course closely linked. The momentum of the forces unleashed by the Prague spring was certainly of a sufficient order to provide a basis for the fears voiced by Ulbricht and Gomulka and by hardliners in the Soviet Politburo, that the Czechoslovak Communist Party might lose control. The fact that many Czechoslovak communists were prepared to accept abandoning their monopoly of power and allowing influence to other forces in society merely aggravated these anxieties. In Poland the possibility that Solidarity might whittle away the authority exercised by the PUWP, and hence its real power, opened up a similar prospect. The fact that the leadership of the Polish party repeatedly stressed its ideological orthodoxy, for instance in maintaining the leading role of the party, offered a certain assurance to the Kremlin and hardliners in the bloc. However, the extent of the actual erosion of the Polish party's authority, and of its vulnerability to non-party pressure, was in marked contrast to the experience of the Czechoslovak party in 1968. Between March and August 1968, the latter had enjoyed a remarkable increase in its popularity; the Polish party could only hope to repair its tarnished image by demonstrating success in terms both of the efficacy of its new economic policies and of its capacity to meet 'social' demands such as the easing of censorship.

The threat to ideological orthodoxy was substantial in both crises. In Czechoslovakia, the reformers' dedication to Marxist socialism was not matched by an equal devotion to Leninism as conceived by the CPSU. The Czech and Slovak reformers had not the slightest intention of restoring capitalism. But the idea of permitting a plurality of interests on an institutionalized basis and of investing the communist party with the role of arbiter between competing interests, rather than that of the exclusive source of influence and power, represented a challenge to Leninism as practised since 1921 in the USSR. In the Polish case, the possibility that forces outside the communist party should be able to extract political as well as economic concessions from the party leadership represented a similar challenge to the Leninist conception of the party's monopoly of power. In both cases the essential feature of 'democratic centralism'—that authority should be transmitted from above but never challenged from below—was at risk.

In Czechoslovakia, the threat to party control was seen as originating within the party leadership itself, carrying the seeds of disintegration of party authority and affording growing opportunities for non-party/counter-revolutionary forces to influence events. In the Soviet perception, the Czechoslovak Communist Party was in the hands of unreliable leaders who could not be trusted to take the necessary action to safeguard the party's continued exercise of power. In Poland, the threat to party control was seen as emanating principally from outside the party leadership, with a spontaneous movement of workers' protest against government failures providing opportunities for 'anti-socialist forces' to subject the communist leadership to intense pressure. It was not until April 1981 that the Soviet Union began to suggest that the Polish party was infiltrated by counter-revolutionary elements. When it then did so, it limited its criticism to the party at large and did not directly criticize the leadership itself.

This difference in the perceived origin and nature of the threat to party control no doubt influenced the Soviet leaders' practical response to the development of the two crises. The majority within the Soviet Politburo evidently reckoned in 1968 that since the Czechoslovak Communist Party was itself inviting a 'creeping counter-revolution', and since the Dubček leadership stubbornly refused to take the drastic 'reverse-engines' type of measure which they deemed necessary, the only satisfactory solution lay in a change of leadership. When it became apparent that this could not be effected by peaceful means, resort was made, albeit with reluctance and misgivings, to military force. The Kremlin's probable assessment that no serious armed resistance would be encountered in Czechoslovakia is likely to have been an important factor in the eventual Soviet decision.[22]

In Poland the different Soviet perception of the origin of the threat helped to explain the apparent Soviet decision, confirmed to Kania during his October 1980 visit to Moscow, to place reliance on the PUWP under its new leadership in steering the country to safety. The Kremlin is also likely to have taken account of the greater likelihood that Poles would put up armed resistance in the event of invasion, and the likely extreme difficulty of 'normalizing' the country after such an event: the likelihood of continuing resistance manifested, for instance, in outbreaks of sabotage (affecting Soviet supply-lines to its troops in the GDR) in a post-invasion scenario may well have been perceived as carrying the risk of necessitating costly military occupation, and very probably military government as well, over a period of years. While all of this must inevitably remain in the realm of speculation, what seems indisputable is that the option of military intervention in Poland would carry greater costs, in terms of its effect on stability (both inside Poland and probably also elsewhere in the bloc) and of likely long-term Soviet military commitments, than did the intervention in Czechoslovakia.

Probably the most striking difference between the two crises lay in the external environment. The increased Soviet stake in détente in 1980 was one consideration favouring caution in the Kremlin; and, unlike

1968 when Western leaders made no serious attempt to deter Soviet military action, in 1980 the NATO alliance made it plain that military intervention in Poland would have grave consequences for détente. The fact that Western public opinion showed much greater interest in the Polish than in the Czechoslovak crisis was of course also relevant. The moral position of the West was stronger than at the time of the Soviet military interventions in either Hungary or Czechoslovakia: whereas the Anglo–French military action in Egypt in 1956 was a source of embarrassment, and in 1968 growing preoccupation with the war in Vietnam influenced the US attitude to the Czechoslovak crisis, in 1980 the boot was on the other foot: the Soviet invasion of Afghanistan had weakened Soviet standing in Third-World countries and also Soviet influence in Western Europe and in many communist parties. It was obvious that military intervention in Poland would cause further erosion of Soviet prestige amongst the neutral and non-aligned, and in the world communist movement.

Economic factors highlighted the Soviet dilemma. The extent of the USSR's interest in 1980 in the economic benefits of détente was illustrated in its negotiation of a huge deal with the FRG and other West European countries, whereby the Soviet Union would obtain vital Western technology for the development of oil and gas resources in exchange for the supply of large quantities of Soviet natural gas. At the same time, the scale of Polish debt represented a special constraint. On the one hand, if Poland was left unmolested, there was a reasonable prospect that Western bankers and governments would provide—albeit reluctantly—enough fresh loans and credits to tide Poland over the next difficult years. On the other hand, in the event of Soviet intervention, there was a clear risk of a drying-up of fresh lending and of the Soviet Union itself being faced with the challenge of servicing and repaying the massive debt.

A further difference in the external environment was that the elaboration of the Brezhnev Doctrine, followed by the inauguration in 1969-70 of an era of détente, had by 1980 created a situation in which non-communist as well as communist forces had a vested interest in détente. Inside Poland, knowledge of the implications of the Brezhnev Doctrine acted as a moderating influence from the early days of the crisis. As early as September, after the signature of the Gdansk agreement, Jacek Kuron spoke of the need to operate 'within the limits set by Soviet tanks'.[23] The Polish Church hierarchy, in line with the Vatican, was acutely conscious of the need for restraint and was evidently not inhibited in using its considerable influence with the Solidarity leaders. In major sermons delivered at moments of particular tension, Cardinal Wyszynski counselled caution and restraint. The Church's attitude was mirrored in the line adopted by Western statesmen who were careful to avoid statements or actions which might encourage opponents of the Polish regime to adopt a more militant stance.[24]

Perhaps the least discouraging aspect of the Polish crisis was the realization in most circles in both East and West that the shared interests still reflected in the concept of détente (even in its post-Afghanistan tarnished state) made the achievement of ideological victories more costly than in previous eras. The least encouraging feature was the fact that the Soviet hold on Eastern Europe—and the Soviet political system itself - still relied heavily on ideological orthodoxy as a principal support (see Chapter 3 on the development of Soviet-East European relations). There was little more sign in 1980 than there had been in 1968 of any Soviet flexibility on basic ideological issues such as a communist party's monopoly of power. It was this feature of the situation which compelled Western governments in 1981 to continue to view with such concern the possibility that resort might yet be made to 1968-type 'fraternal' intervention of one sort of another.

8 Conclusions; the future variables

Over the past three decades, the East European regimes have faced two particularly serious challenges. The first can be described as essentially ideological: the attraction of Western values and especially that of democratic forms of control. The second major challenge has been in the economic sphere: the flawed performance of the governments whose policies are here discussed has given rise to popular discontent and has compounded the political dilemmas. In Hungary, which is outside the immediate scope of this study, the performance of the reformed economy (as of 1968) has evinced many attractive features, and consumer expectations have, to a significant degree, been satisfied. In the German Democratic Republic, similarly good results have been achieved under an administrative-type system, perhaps mainly as a result of a disciplined approach to work. To a lesser degree, the same can be said of the experience of Czechoslovakia, though the Czechoslovak economic system has manifested many weaknesses, not least in the performance of the engineering and other modern industries. At the other end of the spectrum, the Polish authorities failed to evolve a system capable of meeting consumer – and especially working-class – expectations, and committed major planning blunders in their direction of the economy in the 1970s. A particular failure was in not making proper use of the high investment resources obtained from the West. The Romanian case has a number of features similar to the Polish, although so far the leadership's strongly authoritarian style of government has been largely successful in stifling major eruptions of discontent. As in Poland, the industrial workers have shown signs of latent restlessness, and this seems likely to

117

cause the regime increasing anxiety during the 1980s and 1990s.

The ideological challenge was perhaps the most marked in the Czecho-slovak crisis of 1968. While the role of Czechoslovak workers in the 1968 events should not be unduly minimized, the motive force in the Prague spring came from intellectuals and technocrats who saw a limited democratization of political and social life as the means both towards economic efficiency and as a way of ending for ever the authoritarianism characterized in the judicial excesses of the late 1940s and 1950s. The biggest single impact came from the incontrovertible evidence of the failure of the Soviet-style 'command economy' to achieve significant growth in the early and mid-1960s. At the same time, the tradition of independent thinking by Czechoslovak intellectuals was important. This took the form of a growing realization that a model of socialism better suited to a country which was relatively sophisticated and Western-oriented in its economy and in its political culture could be found.

The direct impact of Western influences, and of shifts in the international scene, was probably rather less important in all three countries than local factors, including especially the economic. This would certainly seem to be the case if the somewhat intangible and indirect influence of political culture is excluded. However, external factors have been important in a number of ways. The Czechoslovak reformers were to some extent influenced by Togliatti-style communism in Italy and by the concept of polycentrism. They were also encouraged by the increasing interest being shown in both East and West in détente. Until the elaboration of the Brezhnev Doctrine (and its encapsulation in Brezhnev's speech to the Polish Party Congress in November 1968), it was permissible to hope that a relaxation in East—West tensions would also encompass tolerance of greater latitude in the ideological sphere; the Brezhnev Doctrine reasserted the importance, in Soviet eyes, of a fairly high degree of conformity on basic ideological issues and in respect of political systems. The significant exception was in permitting a degree of experimentation in economic management, provided this did not appear to threaten the political systems. The Hungarians drew considerable benefit from this latitude. The Polish, Czechoslovak and Romanian authorities, in the 1970s, showed only limited interest in economic experimentation, though the reasons for this varied considerably. In Poland, the Gierek regime operated on a basis of considerable weakness, and became increasingly timid in the face of the rebellious attitudes of Polish workers. Half-hearted attempts at price reforms were abandoned in the face of workers' protests. In Czechoslovakia, the close association of ideas for economic reform with political reform in 1962-8 influenced the Husák government to reverse the 1968 economic reforms: such experimentation as has subsequently occurred has been cautious in the extreme. Ceauşescu in Romania has similarly not shown any disposition

118

to experiment with other than administrative-type reforms.

Crystal-ball gazing in the field of international politics is a pastime of limited usefulness: there are so many interconnections and possible permutations that predictions are hazardous. East–West relations are particularly 'accident-prone'. But it may be worth attempting to determine the likely limits of change, and to identify the factors which can be confidently expected to have the greatest influence. The discussion is divided between internal and external factors, and consideration of their possible interaction follows.

The future variables: internal factors

The most serious of the post-war crises in Eastern Europe–the Polish of 1980-81 – was occasioned above all by economic failure; though a workers' sense of alienation, particularly from privileged party and factory bosses, was an important contributory factor. It is obvious that Poland's future stability will depend heavily on a restoration of the economy, and on the authorities being able to induce a return to a proper work spirit. The task of reconstruction is truly massive, despite some promising features (for instance, the prospect of greatly raising agricultural production if a pragmatic and ambitious investment policy is adopted), and overall success will depend on the achievement of a degree of national reconciliation; in 1980 and up to the time of writing in mid-1981, this was hardly yet apparent. A further important factor will be the degree of forbearance which the USSR is prepared to show; the attitude of the hardline East European states, that is Czechoslovakia and the GDR, will also be a factor but a much lesser one.

Possibly the major internal test in Poland will be the success or otherwise of the new economic reform measures planned to come into effect from 1983. If these achieve their highly difficult object of improving efficiency and competitiveness while also ending workers' alienation via co-management, this could transform the Polish economic and political scene. But the process may be very gradual, with the effects not fully felt until after 1985. Almost equally important will be the requirement for the PUWP to find means, for instance via the rotation of offices, of guaranteeing against a repetition of the worst abuses of the 1960s and 1970s.

Neither Czechoslovakia nor Romania face immediate problems of a comparable order in the economic sphere, and there is no sign in them of imminent political crisis. But in the longer term they face problems which are similar to those thrown up in the Polish crisis – in particular the 'alienation' of workers and others outside the party, and the need to improve economic efficiency. Romania's less-developed status probably means that it is not an early candidate for a Polish-type crisis. Czechoslovakia may benefit from the fact that its workforce is more disciplined (and also more easily bought off) than the Polish, but it seems very possible that the Polish virus will infect the intelligentsia particularly in the Czech lands. The 1970s have demonstrated that the employment of rigorous repressive policies can largely stifle protest and prevent any explosions, but whether this is a position which can be easily maintained into the late 1980s and 1990s is another question. External factors may be important here, including not least the denouement of the Polish developments. If there were a shift in the Soviet attitude it would not be difficult to envisage the formation of a Czechoslovak government of a distinctly less conservative tendency than the present one.

The future variables: external factors

(a) The Soviet Union post-Brezhnev

The available evidence about the likely composition of a post-Brezhnev leadership and its likely orientation is, to put it at its highest, patchy: it is certainly not sufficient to permit more than the most speculative treatment. As of early 1981, the most likely scenario for an early succession would appear to be an interim arrangement whereby one or more of the senior members of the present Politburo take over the leadership until the time is judged ripe for a younger generation (now mainly in their fifties) to take up the reins. The second, more definitive succession would be less likely than the first to involve collective leadership. There is little reason to suppose that an interim leadership of one or more of the Kremlin's gerontocrats would be likely to evolve radically new policies in relation to Eastern Europe: the Brezhnev leadership has in many respects been a collective enterprise, and the policy-influencing voices in the new leadership would probably be mostly the same. The possible orientation of a younger leadership is peculiarly difficult to predict, not least because of the difficulty of identifying the most likely candidate(s). Perhaps the area in which a change of approach would emerge least slowly is that of the economy, where there is already a realization in some quarters that decentralizing reforms could bring rewards in efficiency. Still more speculatively, less emphasis might be placed on ideology as a factor for cohesion in Eastern Europe, and greater reliance placed on economic integration as a means of perpetuating an organic relationship with the Soviet Union without requiring an ideological straight-jacket. It seems less likely that a younger leadership would wish to reduce emphasis on military power and strategic advantage as the foundation for the projection of Soviet influence.

120

If this line of speculation is valid, the outcome could be greater diversity in Eastern Europe, with enhanced scope for experimentation and with a broadening of the limits of tolerance. Economic reform would be given impetus, and this could result in a new approach to Comecon integration based on an acceptance of commodity and currency convertibility, along the lines advocated by Hungarian and other East European economists in the 1960s and 1970s. Arguably, this would lead not to a diminution of Comecon integration but to a strengthening of co-operation: trade between member states might be given impetus while formal planning assumed less importance. At the same time, however, it would be likely to work to broad East European advantage in strengthening their competitiveness in industry and hence improving the prospects for mutually beneficial trade with the West.

Such a possible shift in the Soviet approach might have less impact on Romania than on Poland and most other bloc states. Greater Soviet tolerance of diversity would not necessarily imply an acceptance of looser controls in the co-ordination of foreign policy or military policy within the Warsaw Pact framework. The Kremlin could indeed make the maintenance of cohesion in these areas a condition for less uniform patterns of internal development (as, for instance, was the case in Poland in 1956-60 – see Chapter 3). A further point is that it might become more difficult, under this scenario, to maintain in Romania the neo-Stalinist and personalized form of government which forms one of the props of an autonomous foreign policy. If when Ceauşescu eventually steps down collective leadership or some other form of dispersal of central power was to replace personalized control, this would probably serve to increase the opportunities for outside influences to assert themselves in the promotion of bloc co-ordination.

If there is validity in the assumptions made in this study about the past basis of Soviet policy, and in the speculation in this chapter about its future development, there can be little reason to doubt that the Soviet Union would remain prepared to use force as a measure of last resort to prevent a loss of control by a bloc communist party or to ensure the 'reliability' of a communist party leadership, in accordance with the Brezhnev Doctrine. There could, however, be changes in the threshold of Soviet tolerance of a bloc communist party's acceptance of some dilution of its monopoly of power (either of its own volition, as in Czechoslovakia, or under intense pressure, as in Poland). This is a possible conclusion which could be drawn, very tentatively, from the pattern of Soviet responses during the Polish crisis in the second half of 1980 and the first half of 1981. Other important factors would be the Soviet perception of Western reactions and of repercussions in the World Communist Movement (WCM).

(b) Major changes in the World Communist Movement

A gradual further erosion of Soviet influence in the WCM would not necessarily affect Soviet–East European relations. Although this might stimulate Soviet leaders to try to keep a firm ideological grip within the bloc, it would not assist the application of the Brezhnev Doctrine concept of 'fraternal assistance'; maintenance of cohesion through the resort to military force or other forms of overt intervention would be bound to cause further damage to Soviet standing in the WCM. Conversely, the tolerance of diversity in Eastern Europe would help to repair the damage suffered in 1968 and (to a much lesser extent) in 1980 as a result of sabre-rattling during the Polish crisis.

A conceivable Soviet rapprochement with China (though this is becoming increasingly unlikely) could be expected to lead to a somewhat more relaxed Soviet perception of the external threat to security. But there seems little reason to suppose that this would lead to any very substantial downgrading, in Soviet eyes, of the strategic importance of Eastern Europe. The main practical effect might be to release more Soviet resources to strengthening the Warsaw Pact defences, and — just conceivably — to Soviet concurrence with some reduction in the burden falling to the East Europeans.

If a Eurocommunist West European communist party were to achieve power, this would obviously bring the Soviet Union certain benefits, for instance in the inevitable repercussions on the NATO alliance. In Eastern Europe, however, the implications for the Soviet Union could well be adverse. In Poland, for instance, groups enjoying the sympathy of Eurocommunists, such as KOR, could hope for more effective support, including backing at diplomatic level. Such a development might also serve to revive latent revisionist tendencies within the ranks of the East European communist parties.

(c) The vicissitudes of détente

Détente appears to be characterized more by constant ups and downs than by consistency of direction. Attempts to predict its likely course are especially hazardous. For the purpose of this study, let us concentrate on two opposing scenarios: a progressive further deterioration in detente, and its resuscitation.

First, the senario of deterioration. This posits a hardening of attitudes in both West and East, and a return to Cold War approaches. It could stem from a worsening in relations between Super Powers, for instance as a result of a new Soviet 'expansionist' venture in the Third World; from a growth in the influence of the political Right in leading Western states, or from developments in the Eastern bloc itself, for instance a Soviet military intervention in Poland or another bloc state. Variations in origin would affect the extent of the repercussions in Eastern Europe. But the broad lines can be summarized as follows.

An early casualty would almost certainly be the expansion of humanitarian contacts between East and West, ranging from officially sponsored exchanges to private tourism, and the resolution of personal cases and cases of family reunification. It seems probable that all bloc countries would adopt significantly harder positions in these areas; the effects on the policies of Western governments would be likely to be smaller, given their lesser preoccupation with the security implications of human interchange. But a certain hardening of approach would probably ensue in such spheres as visa-issuing practices and in the provision of government support for cultural exchanges with the East.[1] Within the bloc, the effects would be greatest in the most 'liberal' countries, notably Poland and Hungary. In Czechoslovakia, many of the Czechoslovak government's existing policies might be thought to require little or no modification—for instance, the exceptionally stringent controls restricting exit from the country. In Poland on the other hand it seems hard to conceive of the continuation, in a Cold War scenario, of the relatively relaxed approach of the authorities to personal travel. The permitted rate of emigration of special groups, such as ethnic Germans and Jews, would be likely to suffer, though in the case of the Germans there would be the consolation that a large proportion of those wishing to leave Poland and some of those wishing to leave Romania have already been able to do so.

East European governments might fear the consequences for internal stability of any switch on the part of Western broadcasting services to a more aggressive approach, and there might be a general resumption of jamming. Although Western broadcasts, particularly those of Radio Free Europe, have already been subject to much denunciation in Eastern media, the real concern of the regimes is likely to have been less with the foreign broadcasting stations' alleged encouragement for the activities of subversive groups than with their purveying information about the actual situation in these territories which they would prefer not to be divulged. No Western broadcasting service has in recent times engaged in direct support for opposition groups. It would be possible to imagine a less restrained approach in the event of a return to the atmosphere of the Cold War (though Western governments would doubtless remain concerned to observe to the letter the Principle of Non-Intervention in the Helsinki Final Act).[2] On the Eastern side, an obvious early target for punitive action would be Western journalists; again the impact might be much greater in Poland, where foreign journalists in 1980/81 enjoyed considerable latitude, than in Czechoslovakia, where these activities had been tightly restricted.

In the economic sphere, a hardening of East—West relations might have less serious effects on Eastern Europe than on the Soviet Union: the Afghanistan affair demonstrated that a major setback in Soviet-Western relations need not necessarily carry penalties in Eastern Europe commensurate with those in the USSR. The West's 'differentiated approach' enabling 'business as usual' to proceed, in the wake of the invasion of Afghanistan, with the majority of East European states was on the whole well received in Eastern Europe. It was also found that the post-Afghanistan tightening of the strategic embargo via Comecon had relatively little impact on Comecon states other than the Soviet Union. The West might be expected to act similarly in the event of a new Soviet adventure in which Eastern Europe was at most indirectly involved. On the other hand, Soviet military intervention in a bloc state which led to a tightening of the Soviet grip on bloc affairs would no doubt evoke a more uniform type of Western response with a lesser tendency to differentiate between 'liberal' and 'illiberal' states. So far as credit policies are concerned, the first casualties would be likely to be government-backed credits and government loans; credits by private banks would however certainly also be affected. The various factors which have influenced the huge scale of bank loans to Poland have included the political judgement that Poland is a particularly deserving bloc country with a relatively good recent record in the realm of humanitarian contacts and human rights.

A return to the Cold War, whatever its origin, would inevitably have an impact on the internal policies of bloc governments, and doubtless also on the course of bloc integration. The auguries for decentralizing economic reforms would not be good, and some of the advances already made – notably in Hungary – could be put at risk. If, as would appear likely in the envisaged contingency, the Soviet Union were to press for more far-reaching integration of the Comecon economies, this would militate in favour of those demanding a high degree of centralization to the exclusion of market forces. At the same time, a more uniform approach to dissidents could well emerge. The Czechoslovak government's approach to dissidents may be reckoned to come close already to fitting a Cold War scenario. A similar (and indeed *harsher*) comment could be made about Romania, notwithstanding its better international image. The effects in Poland, where hitherto a degree of dissent has been tolerated as a kind of safety-valve for social pressures, would be likely to be more serious. Given the degree of social self-expression already achieved, and the high expectations which have been engendered in 1980/81, it is not difficult to conceive of a situation in which the leadership would judge the only safe option to be the institution of a highly repressive form of government. This might be combined with some form of 'fraternal' assistance.

In the realm of foreign policy, Romania would be the bloc state most obviously vulnerable to a Cold War scenario. If the CSCE process were to collapse, this would put an end to the Romanian aspirations for a Europe based not on military blocs but on the principles of sovereign equality and non-intervention. Romanian freedom of manoeuvre would in any event be likely to suffer, with economic pressures towards Comecon integration and military pressures for closer Warsaw Pact co-ordination supplementing the centripetal political pressures. Poland and Czechoslovakia would be less affected since their freedom of manoeuvre in foreign policy is already heavily circumscribed. It may be recalled (see Chapter 4) that Poland took foreign policy initiatives before the era of detente which were comparable to the recent proposal for a European Conference on Disarmament.

Now let us turn to the more optimistic scenario of a resuscitation of détente. In the short term, a return to the heady atmosphere of 1973-5 seems hardly likely, since the disillusionment with détente which set in at the end of the 1970s was more than an ephemeral mood: it reflected the sober realization that the concept of a cordial, non-antagonist relationship between East and West had taken little account of the realities of Soviet motivations. These realities were spelt out clearly enough in Brezhnev's speech to the Twenty-fifth Party Congress in February 1976 when he stated that peaceful coexistence, far from ending the class struggle, created better opportunities for the triumph of socialism; détente did not mean a relaxation, but rather an intensification, of the ideological struggle. It was not, however, until the invasion of Afghanistan in December 1979 that the full implications of this simple message were fully absorbed by Western publics and governments. If détente is to be resuscitated, it is likely to reflect in the West a more hard-headed view of the limits of co-operation between antagonistic political and ideological systems.

The likely gains for Poland and Romania following an improvement in the East-West climate are not hard to discern. In Poland, the chances would improve for political stabilization of a kind which would allow leeway for non-communist elements in society, and permit the relaxation of authoritarian controls. Although the advantage here might be thought to accrue more to non-communists than to the ruling PUWP, it would be considered preferable by many communists to the alternative of harsh repression (discussed above in the 'collapse of detente' scenario). Contacts with the West would flourish and in the economic sphere there would be obvious benefits for the government as well as for ordinary Poles: the climate would be improved for the extension of Western economic support, including the agreement of new measures to ease the servicing and repayment of Polish debts, which constitute a highly desirable ingredient of economic recovery. Where the effects of a resuscitation of détente are less easy to assess is in the area of individual liberties and the toleration of freedom of speech. Some of the adverse effects of the previous scenario of a reversion to Cold War attitudes would certainly seem likely to be avoided. However, the Polish authorities have shown anxiety about the perceived ways in which détente in the 1970s appeared to encourage and assist opposition forces aiming (as they see it) to construct a new balance of forces within the state. PUWP leaders might well conclude that, if détente is revived in the 1980s, barriers must be constructed to limit the extent of ideological contamination from the West.

In Czechoslovakia, the resuscitation of détente would render more difficult a continuation of the hardline approach to internal criticism and dissent which has characterized 'normalization'. The most immediate effect might be to encourage pragmatists in the Czechoslovak Politburo and Central Committee who would prefer to pursue less dogmatic and intolerant policies, and who are attracted by the idea of instituting decentralizing economic reforms in order to improve efficiency and performance. As regards Romania, the experience of the 1970s offers little to suggest that a resuscitation of detente would have a major impact on internal policies. The latter have evidently been determined much more by domestic considerations, by Ceauşescu's commitment to rapid industrial growth, and by the influence of developments in the bloc (notably in 1980-81 in Poland), than by any Western influences. In foreign affairs, the obverse of the previous scenario would apply: the scope for autonomy in foreign policy would be enlarged.

If the assumption is valid that Western attitudes to détente will be more realistic than those of the mid-1970s, there may be constraining effects on Soviet behaviour. The Kremlin may be more prepared to pay heed to the repercussions on Western policy-makers of actions construed in the West to be expansionist, or to be narrowly based on the preponderance of military power. Such considerations would militate against armed intervention in a bloc state although, as discussed above, the decisive ultimate consideration would be likely to be the degree of perceived threat to Soviet national security.

(d) A breakthrough in arms control and negotiations affecting Central Europe

It is beyond the scope of this study to speculate about the many types of reductions in armament in the Central European area which might result from a breakthrough in the MBFR talks in Vienna, SALT-3 talks on medium-range missiles, etc. It is obvious that progress in this area would help to overcome Western disillusionment with the results of detente, and would contribute to the realization of the second scenario discussed above. It would doubtless also be welcomed in Eastern as well as Western Europe as a path to the reduction of military spending. But there is little evidence suggesting that negotiated troop reductions in the central theatre, or reductions in deployment of tactical and medium-range missiles, would be likely to result in any fundamental changes in Soviet-East European relations. It is hard to envisage circumstances in which the Kremlin would contemplate the withdrawal of all its conventional forces from East Germany, Czechoslovakia and Poland and, even if this were to happen, Soviet military power would remain a powerful political factor affecting Eastern Europe. There is no reason to suppose that the Soviet leaders would, as a result, lose interest in maintaining the cohesion of the 'socialist commonwealth' and its ideological integrity. As argued in Chapter 3, the ideological links are of a fundamental importance since they affect, amongst other things, the legitimation of communist party rule in the Soviet Union itself.

Convergence or isolation?

The discussion in Chapter 3 has suggested that the 'Finlandization' of Eastern Europe is hardly a realistic prospect in the foreseeable future. If, as would now seem most likely, the trend in the 1980s is towards carefully controlled and restricted co-operation between an East and a West which both recognize the antagonistic basis on which this coexistence seems doomed to rest, the evolution of Eastern Europe in the direction of greater autonomy and national self-expression may be a slow process. The 1968 Soviet intervention in Czechoslovakia had a retarding impact on the cause of reform (from within communist parties) not only in Czechoslovakia, but also elsewhere in the bloc. If the Polish experiment is crushed by repressive means, this will retard the possibilities everywhere for the expression of discontent outside party fora.

If, conversely, the Polish experiment succeeds in the sense that a restoration of the economy is accompanied by the observance of social and political arrangements which give a voice to all (other than right-wing) forces in society, this may well encourage other similar trends elsewhere. In the medium term, Czechoslovakia would be a candidate and so, probably, would the GDR. In Romania, the influence might be more easily contained, given the disruption of organized opposition there. For the Soviet Union, the principal worry would naturally concern the cohesion of the bloc, and Soviet ability to retain sufficient instruments of control.

Taking a historical view, there would certainly seem to be discernible a long-term trend working towards the convergence of Eastern and Western Europe, particularly in the cultural realm, and in the field of ideas. Evidence of this could be seen in both the Czechoslovak crisis of 1968 and the Polish troubles beginning in 1980. Unless this trend can be somehow accommodated with the Soviet Union's insistence on controls which are (in large part) ideologically based, the outcome in the short run is most likely to be the institution of new barriers, both ideological and physical. In the long run, one may only hope that the Soviet Union will itself adapt.

So far as Western policy is concerned, the Polish crisis appeared to demonstrate that a mixture of Western restraint (in, for instance, eschewing interference in Polish affairs) and firmness *vis-à-vis* the USSR (for instance, the 20 December 1980 NATO communiqué) could pay good dividends. In future crises, it must be hoped that Western governments show similar firmness and community of outlook.

For the Soviet Union, the greatest worry for the future must be that ideas have no barriers. Marxism is a philosophy posited on a constant struggle between opposites, and on constant changes through the dialectical process. This basic aspect of the philosophy appears to be thought no longer relevant to the Soviet Union in view of its progress in the construction of socialism. In Eastern Europe, whatever the position in theory, the struggle between different sets of ideas and values is in practice very far from over, and it may cause much further instability. It constitutes, in effect, one of the world's principal danger-points and one of the main incentives for the Soviet Union on the one hand, and the major Western nations on the other, to strive to rebuild the rules of coexistence on a new and more realistic basis.

Postscript

The imposition of martial law on the night of 12–13 December 1981 appeared to dash all hope in Poland of achieving, in the foreseeable future, a degree of political pluralism. How far does this development weaken the proposition that Eastern Europe's opening to the West should lead towards political liberalization as well as producing material benefits?

The Polish experience of 1970–82 was peculiar in the sense that massive borrowing in the West served to shore up an incompetent political leadership without providing any very obvious tangible benefits. At the same time the influences associated with détente and the Helsinki Final Act helped to encourage opponents and critics of the Polish regime, and to generate powerful pressures for a radical and rapid transformation of the system. The result was an unhappy mix of economic collapse and social and political turmoil. The outcome has in fact followed the pattern of previous major East European crises – Hungary 1956, Czechoslovakia 1968 – when military power was used to suppress forces which appeared to threaten the kernel of the political system. The difference of course is that actual Soviet military intervention has, in the case of Poland, so far been avoided.

The recent Polish experience reinforces the view of those who believe that progress in Eastern Europe is more likely to come through evolution than by rapid and dramatic means. It has also demonstrated how relatively limited is the scope for the West to influence events when dramatic change occurs.

It may be argued that Western actions, such as NATO warnings in

1980–81, helped to prevent a Soviet military invasion of Poland. This may well be so, although probably the most fundamental factor in the dénouement was the gravity of the economic crisis, coupled with the failure of the PUWP and of Solidarity to find solutions through negotiation. It may also be argued that Western actions post-December 1981, such as the measures announced by member states of NATO and others in January and February 1982, have been useful in reminding the Soviet Union and the Polish government of the linkage between détente and respect for human rights. But as the Western countries recognized themselves, such measures could not induce a return to 'renewal' in Poland. There was indeed the risk that sanctions which seriously hurt Poland's economy might delay, not advance, the ending of martial law.

The impact of Western, and CSCE-type, influences is a cumulative one, over a long term. As noted, they certainly contributed to the recent Polish events. The do not, so far, appear to have had radical effects within the Soviet Union itself, and there is little evidence that the Brezhnev leadership has in any way revised the thinking behind the Brezhnev Doctrine. Yet, as *Pravda* might say, life itself will induce changes in time. These changes will be influenced partly by the need for the Soviet Union to maintain coexistence and economic links with the West. But they will be influenced above all by the fundamental weaknesses in communist systems which both Czechoslovakia in 1968, and Poland in 1980–82, have demonstrated so vividly. These weaknesses, which are especially damaging in the economic field, are the subject of increasing attention within the World Communist Movement. Although the Soviet leadership has so far appeared to pay little heed to Eurocommunist criticism, future Soviet leaders will have to take into account the extent to which the existing Soviet model of socialism is a source of economic weakness as well as of vulnerability in the WCM.

It may be that new forms of economic management, perhaps borrowing from both the Hungarian and the Yugoslav experience, will be found as a way of staving off social and political discontent. In Poland the Jaruzelski regime would certainly not appear to have lost interest in this aspect of 'renewal'. But, without some movement on the political front, this may not be enough to avert future disasters. Unless independent institutions in society are given a role, there will be no effective means of limiting the errors of decision-makers in the 'socialist' states. As Wlodimierz Brus has suggested, the absence of any feedback mechanism is a source of weakness equal to the refusal to allow scope to market forces in the economy.[1]

The setback in Poland has encouraged some members of the European Left to revive ideas of a solution along Rapacki Plan lines which, by reducing military tension in central Europe, would give political pluralism in Eastern Europe a fairer wind.[2] Although this is an idea which, in the right circumstances, would have a certain appeal, there is little sign of any present Soviet willingness to consider the kind of concessions which would make it palatable to Western policy-makers. The progress to date in MBFR is hardly an encouraging portent. If a more experimentally inclined Soviet leadership emerges, the idea could well receive greater attention.

Meanwhile, much patience may be needed. My own view remains that practical East—West co-operation will continue to offer rewards, certainly in the medium term, and that, of the various ways forward, ideological warfare is the least promising. The West can derive both comfort and optimism from the fact that the most penetrating criticism of the East European systems now comes from within the communist movement itself.

February 1982.

Notes

1 Introduction

1 See Preface, Z. Brzezinski, *The Soviet Bloc*, rev. edn (Harvard Univ. Press, Cambridge, Mass., 1967)

2 This is argued especially convincingly in Stephen White, *Political Culture and Soviet Politics* (Macmillan, London, 1979).

3 An excellent, scholarly analysis of this disparity is to be found in Archie Brown and Jack Gray (eds), *Political Culture and Political Change in Community States* (Macmillan, London, 1977).

2 The evolution of the regimes

1 Hugh Seton-Watson, *The East European Resolution* (Methuen, London, 3rd edn 1956) gives probably the best general account.

2 See Paul Lendvai, *Eagles and Cobwebs* (Macdonald, London, 1970) pp. 288-9.

3 See Chapter 3.

4 The riots were, on all the evidence, entirely spontaneous. See for example Adam Bromke, *Poland's Politics: Idealism vs. Realism*

(Harvard Univ. Press, Cambridge, Mass., 1967) p. 97.

5   A comparison can be drawn between the Romanian leadership's ambitious approach to industrialization and the policy adopted by Stalin in the Soviet Union in 1928, which was accompanied by enforced collectivization. In the Romanian case, however, collect-ivization was achieved more gradually.

6   See for example V.V. Kusin in R. Tokes (ed.), *Opposition in Eastern Europe* (Macmillan, London, 1979) pp. 60-85.

7   See Z. Mlynar, *Night Frost in Prague* (Methuen, London, 1980) pp.   .

8   Public opinion polls in the spring and summer of 1968 revealed a considerable degree of public trust in the reform leadership, and testified to Dubček's undoubted popularity. See H. Gordon Skilling, *Czechoslovakia's Interrupted Revolution* (Princeton Univ. Press, Princeton, N.J., 1976) pp. 534-42.

9   The circumstances of Ceauşescu's consolidation of his personal power is described in Lendvai, *Eagles and Cobwebs*, pp. 318-20. Ironically, one of the ruses employed was to pose as a champion of 'collective leadership' and of the strict separation of state and party posts.

10 Reference was made to the need for co-operation with socialist countries in a spirit of socialist internationalism 'without specific mention of any individual countries' (Article 14). In 1960, Czecho-slovakia had been authorized to emulate the USSR in achieving full socialism with the proclamation of a constitution proclaiming itself 'socialist'. Romania on the other hand made the change without permission and at a stage of development when the use of the term would not have been considered appropriate by the USSR.

11 See Chapter 4.

12 See on this Brzezinski, *The Soviet Bloc.*

13 Quoted in P. Raina, *Political Opposition in Poland 1954-1978* (Poets and Painters Press, London, 1977) p. 200.

14 Problems over minorities have remained an irritant in relations between bloc countries. The treatment of Hungarian minorities in

both Romania and (to a lesser extent) Czechoslovakia continues to occasion some friction. But it is not an issue which poses a major internal challenge to the regimes.

15 The Romanian idiosyncrasies are well described in K.R. Jowitt, 'Political Innovation in Romania', *Survey*, vol. 20, no. 4 (Autumn 1974).

16 See G. Kolankiewicz in D. Lane and G. Kolankiewicz (eds), *Social Groups in Polish Society* (Macmillan, London, 1973) p. 114.

17 ibid., p. 150.

18 *Polityka* of 25 December 1976, quoted in Raína, *Political Opposition in Poland 1954-1978*. p. 411.

19 Jerzy Urban in, *Polityka* of 22 November 1980.

3   The development of Soviet policy towards Eastern Europe

1   J. Wszelaki, *Communist Economic Strategy: The Role of East Central Europe* (Washington, 1959) pp. 68-77.

2   N. Khrushchev, *Khrushchev Remembers* (André Deutsch, London, 1974) pp. 194-207.

3   V. Mićunović, *Moscow Diary* (Chatto & Windus, London, 1980) p. 213.

4   Khrushchev, *Khrushchev Remembers*.

5   Khrushchev's acknowledgement of 'different roads' to socialism in his Twentieth Party Congress speech was much qualified in later Soviet pronouncements. Suslov's view that the shift to socialism takes place on a 'mainly uniform and common road', with variations only in the forms and methods used, acquired increasing weight in Soviet interpretations, See Boris Meissner, *The Brezhnev Doctrine* Park College, Mo., 1970) pp. 13-15.

6   Text from William E. Griffith, *Sino-Soviet Relations 1964-1965* MIT Press, Cambridge, Mass., 1967) p. 284. Quoted in Kenneth

Jowitt, *Revolutionary Breakthroughs and National Development, The Case of Romania* (Univ. of California Press, Berkeley, 1971).

7   Jowitt, *Revolutionary Breakthroughs*, 234-5.

8   Thomas A. Wolfe, *Soviet Power and Europe 1945-1970* (Johns Hopkins Press, Baltimore, 1970) pp. 307-8.

9   See text of press conference by General Prchlik, 1968, in Skilling, *Czechoslovakia's Interrupted Revolution*.

10 See Chapters 6 and 7 below.

11 For a recent account of the meaning and continuing implications of the Brezhnev Doctrine, see my chapter 'The Continuing Validity of the Brezhnev Doctrine', in Karen Dawisha and Philip Hanson (eds), *Soviet—East European Dilemmas: Coercion, Competition, and Consent* (Heinemann/RIIA, London, 1981), pp. 26–40.

12 Mlynar, *Night Frost in Prague*, pp. 238-40.

13 This is one of the key principles of the Brezhnev Doctrine as enunciated by Kovalev in *Pravda*, 26 September 1968: 'The weakening of any link in the world socialist system has a direct effect on all the socialist countries, which cannot be indifferent to this ... World socialism as a social system is the common achievement of the working people of all counties, it is indivisible, and its defence is the common cause of all communists ...'

14 The most immediate Soviet worry in the summer of 1968 appears to have centred on the possible effects of the Czechoslovak deviation on the stability of the Ukraine, where the local party boss Shelest was reportedly uneasy. For a fuller analysis of Soviet motivations, see Chapter 6.

15 While it can be argued that Romania has proved an exception to the rule, it is likely that Soviet leaders are apprehensive above all at the possibility that spontaneous forces in a bloc state, unsympathetic to the Soviet Union, might affect that state's reliability in the Eastern alliance. This certainly was a major preoccupation in 1968.

16 Paul Marer in C. Gati (ed.), *The International Politics of Eastern Europe* (Praeger, New York, 1976).

17 The most authoritative recent manual would appear to be Sh. P. Sanakoyev (ed.), *Socialism: Foreign Policy in Theory and Practice* (Progress Publishers, Moscow, 1976).

18 ibid., p. 64. The Sanakoyev manual also claims, interestingly, that 'the national interests of any socialist country ... are organically fused with its internationalist interests' (p. 81).

4 The opening to the exterior

1 Bromke, *Poland's Politics*, p. 133.

2 *Pravda*, 8 May 1958, quoted in ibid., p. 135.

3 Examples of optimistic views are to be found in Adam Bromke and John W. Strong, *Gierek's Poland* (Praeger, New York/London, 1973). For a more critical evaluation, see Alex Pravda, 'Gierek's Poland: five years on', *The World Today*, July 1976; and Adam Bromke, 'Poland at the crossroads', ibid., April 1978. In fact, the claimed increases in 'real wages' were in large part illusory, since the supply of goods failed to meet demand and shortages increased dramatically.

4 There is some evidence that, up to 1964, the USSR was seriously interested in the possibility of progressively demilitarizing non-Soviet Eastern Europe with a view, amongst other things, to allowing a certain elbow room for Poland and other East European states. The Brezhnev leadership discarded this option, switching to a policy of closing all the power gaps which might have existed in Eastern Europe in preparation for CSCE talks. See contribution by A.J. Liehm, quoting Polish Foreign Ministry sources, in V. Kusin (ed.), The Czechoslovak Reform Movement 1968 *(International Research Documents,* London, 1973).

5 Bromke, *Poland's Politics*, p. 240.

6 Quoted in Sanakoyev, *Socialism: Foreign Policy in Theory and Practice*, p. 81.

7 Difficulty in obtaining the necessary hard currency has however been a persistent problem which continues in practice to deter many potential visitors to the West.

8 R. Remington (ed.), *Winter in Prague* (MIT Press, Cambridge, Mass., 1969) p. 121.

9   ibid., p. 134.

10 Quoted in ibid., pp. 213-23.

11 For a discussion of Soviet attitudes to economic reform, see W. Brus, *Soviet-East European Dilemmas* (Heinemann, London, 1981).

12 While the figure of Czechs and Slovaks visiting the West is nearly as high as that for Poles visiting the West, such comparisons are somewhat misleading since a very high proportion of the Czechoslovak total comprises border crossings to neighbouring (neutral) Austria; Poland has no Western neighbour.

13 A good recent summary is Robert R. King, 'Romania's Struggle for an Autonomous Foreign Policy', *The World Today*, August 1979.

14 Romania's legislation permitting participation by foreign capital in ventures in Romania (up to 49 per cent) was the first to be introduced in the Soviet bloc. To date, only Hungary has followed the Romanian example.

15 The treaty, while the result of Soviet pressure, contained one consolation: unlike the 1970 Soviet-Czechoslovak Friendship Treaty of the same year, it did not contain any Brezhnev Doctrine-type formulations.

16 The one exception was an explicit reference by Ceauşescu to the Soviet Union as one of the culprits in Afghanistan in an article published in a Swedish journal at the time of the Romanian President's visit to Sweden in November 1980.

17 The scant military attention paid by the Russians to Romania is described in the paper by Professor John Erickson in Kusin, *The Czechoslovak Reform Movement 1968*, p. 34.

18 The fusion of state and party offices in 1972 marked a departure from Soviet practice which was difficult to reconcile with ideological orthodoxy (see K.R. Jowitt in *Survey*, Autumn 1973). But the practical result was to strengthen the party leaders' control, in contrast to the heresies of Czechoslovak reformers which had threatened to dilute it.

5 The economic outlook

1   In *Zycie Gospodarcze* no. 38, 21 September 1980.

2   See for example the report in *The Times* of 23 September 1980 that trials involving economic crimes, including bribery of foreign trade officials, were being launched. The head of Minex was amongst those accused.

3   Figure was quoted by Mieszczanowski in *Zycie Gospodarcze*.

4   A major Western bank credit of $325 million was granted in July 1980, after the work stoppages had started. In September, the United States pledged a 20 per cent increase for 1981 in credits for grain purchases (totalling $690 million). *New York Times*, 14 September 1980.

5   *Guardian*, 5 September 1980.

6   Figures given in *The Times*, 14 October 1980.

7   Report by Strougal at Eighteenth Session of CPC Central Committee, Rudo Pravo, 15 October 1980.

8   Address by Foreign Trade Minister Barcak to diplomatic representatives in Prague. *Prace*, 30 January 1980.

9   *Radio Free Europe*, vol. 5, no. 35 (14-19 August 1980), quoting V. Bilak in *Tribuna*, 21 May 1980.

10 *Neue Zuercher Zeitung*, 24 May 1979.

11 It has been rumoured that the Adria pipeline will be used in the reverse direction, viz. to supply Soviet crude to Yugoslavia (which is unable to buy the OPEC crude it had expected to use as feedstock for its petrochemicals plant at Krk).

12 Paper by Anthony Scanlon delivered at NATO Symposium, April 1980.

13 For example, the complaint reported in *The Times* of 29 September 1980 of dumping of Czechoslovak clocks in the UK at prices 30 per cent below British wholesale prices.

14 See Note 7.

15 Speech to workers reported in *Scinteia*, 14 June 1980.

16 'Romania: the Industrialization of an Agrarian Economy under Socialist Planning', The World Bank, Washington, D.C., 1979.

17 ibid.

18 *East-West Trade and Indebtedness in the Seventies and Eighties*, Centralsparkasse und Kommerzbank, Vienna, 1978.

19 W. Brus in *Soviet Studies*, vol. XXXI, no. 2 (April 1979).

20 This point is among many aspects of Polish indebtedness ably analysed by Richard Portes in *The Polish Crisis: Western Economic Policy Options* (Royal Institute of International Affairs, London 1981). Portes recommends that the Polish programme for economic reform be monitored year by year, and that satisfactory progress should be a precondition for the provision of new funds.

6 The Competing Pulls: the Internal Political Scene

1 See Brown and Gray (eds), *Political Culture and Political Change*, p. 107.

2 Quoted in Raína, *Political Opposition in Poland*, p. 179.

3 Bromke, *Poland's Politics*, p. 229.

4 A good summary of KOR's development is in Jacques Rupnik, 'Dissent in Poland, 1968-79: the End of Revisionism and the Rebirth of Civil Society', in Tokes (ed.), *Opposition in Eastern Europe*.

5 *Le Monde*, 2 September 1980.

6 *Sztandar Mlodych*, 9 September 1980.

7 Raína, *Political Opposition in Poland*, p. 283.

8 Contained in *Sztandar Mlodych*, 9 September 1980.

9 Based on a firsthand account from a Western consular official serving in a Baltic seaboard city.

10 In interviews with Western journalists, Walesa was not reticent in offering comment on developments in the West; one of his more surprising observations was that Britain had become 'too rich'. His vision of a regenerated Poland as a 'new Japan' encountered criticism - and some scepticism!

11 Quoted in *Rude Pravo*, 26 March 1980.

12 The Covenants had been signed by Czechoslovakia in 1968 during Dubček's tenure of the First Secretaryship; their ratification in 1976 was a logical, though not strictly necessary, complement to Czechoslovakia's signature of the Final Act.

13 Zdenek Mlynar, one of the leading Czech reformers who went into exile, attempted to mobilize Eurocommunist support in the early 1970s but was disappointed by the results. At the 1976 Conference of European Communist Parties, 'normalization' in Czechoslovakia was touched upon only in passing in one speech - that of Berlinguer. See Kusin in Tokes (ed.), *Opposition in Eastern Europe*, p. 49.

14 There have been rumours that the meeting between the Czechoslovak and Hungarian leaderships in November 1980 revealed misgivings about the dogmatism of Bilak-style policies. (Private information from Hungarian sources.)

15 Amnesty International Report on Romania. London, 1979.

7   Czechoslovakia 1968, Poland 1980: the international dimension

1   While there is no evidence that *Polityka* was directly involved in this, perhaps the best example of reformist tendencies within the party were the reports of the 'Experience and the Future' group, which included both communists and non-communists.

2   Although the Kania Politburo contained some figures who espoused limited economic reform, e.g. Olszowski, no one within it was known to have any personal commitment to democratization or to substantial relaxation of controls.

3   R. Selucky, in *Problems of Communism*, vol. XXIV, (Jan-Feb 1975) pp. 38-43.

4   Skilling, *Czechoslovakia's Interrupted Revolution*, p. 832.

5 Remington (ed.), *Winter in Prague*, pp. 87-8.

6 See for example report in *Financial Times* of 18 December 1980. 'Reliable' sources in Moscow were said to have described the purposes of the meeting of bloc leaders in Moscow on 5 December as being to 'formalize' the pledge of support Kania was given in Moscow in October. The contrast with Bratislava where bloc leaders pressurized Dubček is obvious.

7 Address to party meeting in Gdansk as quoted in *Rude Pravo* of 10 November 1980.

8 *Polityka*, no. 82, 18 October 1980.

9 Dawisha, *Soviet-East European Dilemmas*.

10 Speech at Gera, 13 October 1980, reported in *SWB*, 15 October 1980.

11 Speech reported in *SWB*, 9 October 1980.

12 Address to mid-October Plenum of Romanian Communist Party, quoted in *Sztandar Mlodych* (Warsaw), no. 252, 21 October 1980.

13 For example, the report (*Le Monde*, 18 August 1980) of a stoppage of work for several hours by 2,000-3,000 workers in Tirgovişte against 'persistent shortage of meat'. Meat was said to have thereupon immediately appeared.

14 TASS report of 8 December 1980, carried in *SWB*, 9 December 1980.

15 TASS, 29 November 1980, monitored in *SWB*, 2 December, quoting *Rude Pravo*, 27 November.

16 Report in *The Times*, 17 December 1980, of Boris Ponomaryov's statement to M. Chaban-Delmas, on the occasion of a Soviet parliamentary visit to Paris.

17 Text for Moscow Home Service report, quoted in *SWB*, 21 October 1980.

18 The most frequently cited allegation was of an AFL/CIO grant to Polish unions of $25,000 in early September. *Pravda* significantly

attacked the alleged links between Western and Polish unions immediately *after* the Gdansk Agreement had been signed.

19 *The Times*, 12 December 1980.

20 While the independent unions' and Solidarity's main preoccupation was with trade union rights, it was also concerned with the defence of more broadly conceived human rights. This was reflected in the inclusion in the Szczecin Protocol of the demand that the UN Human Rights Convention, and the Helsinki Final Act, be *again* published in Poland. *Glos Pracy*, 2 September 1980, quoted in *SWB* 11 September 1980.

21 For detailed account of Western communist parties' reaction, see Appendix III, *The Strikes in Poland* (RFE Research, Munich, October 1980).

22 While there is no direct evidence of Soviet calculations on this question, the fact that the Czechoslovak leadership did not seriously entertain the option of military resistance at the time of the invasion suggests that the margin of doubt is unlikely to have been very great.

23 *Daily Telegraph*, 2 September 1980.

24 East Europeans were much less worried by the attitudes and pro-nouncements of Western statesmen than by the 'hysterical' coverage of Polish developments by Western media which, it was feared, might exacerbate tensions in Poland and elsewhere.

8 Conclusions: the future variables

1 The scale of financial support by most Western governments for cultural exchanges with East European countries has however so far not been very substantial.

2 As with many provisions of the Helsinki Final Act, there is a marked difference between Western and Eastern interpretations of this Principle. In the Western view, its intention is to preclude overt intervention, especially intervention involving physical force, but *not* to preclude criticism of internal practices of member states, for instance in the media of another state.

142

Postscript

1   In his interesting contribution to the Round Table discussion on 'Socialist Economies in the World' in *Marxism Today*, February 1982.

2   See, in particular the article by E.P. Thompson in *The Times*, 22 February 1982.

Index

China, 42, 47–51, 122
  Sino–Soviet dispute, 20–1, 28, 46, 122
Church in Poland, 6–7, 9, 15, 21, 82, 84–6, 96, 115
Conference on Security and Co-operation in Europe, 23–5, 32, 45, 103–4, 125
  Final Act, 24, 41, 49, 52–3, 82–3, 85–8, 91, 94–5, 111–12, 123, 139 n.2
Council for Mutual Economic Assistance (COMECON), 20, 22, 33, 62, 121, 124
  Comprehensive Programme of Integration, 25–6, 32–3, 56, 103
  Czechoslovakian view of, 63–5, 73
  negotiations with EEC, 53, 74
  Romanian view of, 46, 50, 72, 104
Cuban missile crisis, 20, 22, 38
currency convertibility, 75, 121

Declaration of Independence in Czechoslovakia, 21–2, 47
Dubček, A., 9, 11, 15, 24, 30, 44, 51, 97–9, 105, 107–8, 112, 114, 130 n.8

European Community (EEC), 26, 48, 53–4, 62
  negotiations with Comecon, 53, 74

Federal Republic of Germany, 23–6, 35–6, 40, 42–5, 47–8, 62, 81, 91, 103, 110
Finland, 33
France, 23, 39, 47–8, 92–3

Gaulle, President C. de, 39, 47
Genscher, H.D., 107
German Democratic Republic, 18, 20, 55, 105–6, 110, 117, 119, 127
  international recognition, 23–4
Gheorghiu-Dej, G., 5, 7–9, 11, 13–14, 21, 46, 51
Gierek, E., 5, 12–17, 36–7, 39–41, 56–7, 75–6, 79, 85–6, 95, 97, 102, 118
Giscard d'Estaing, V., 39
Goma, P., 91
Gomulka, W., 5–6, 9, 12–13, 15, 19, 21, 29, 36–41, 76, 79–81, 98, 106, 113
Gomulka Plan, 38
Gottwald, K., 7, 10
Group of 77, 47, 51

Helsinki Final Act *see* Conference on Security and Co-operation in Europe
Honecker, E., 106
Hua Guofeng, 47, 50
human and cultural contacts, 45, 52–5, 105–6, 123, 134 n.12; *in*
  Czechoslovakia, 45, 52, 87
  Poland, 40–1, 52, 79, 86
  Romania, 55, 91
human rights, 112, 125–6, 139 n.20; *in*
  Czechoslovakia, 45, 88–9
  Poland, 82–3, 85
  Romania, 91
Hungary, 6–7, 11, 18–20, 35, 87, 117–18, 124
Husák, G., 10–11, 44–5, 88, 90, 106–7, 118

Indra, A., 11
International Bank for Reconstruction and Development (IBRD), 47–8, 70–2
International Monetary Fund (IMF), 47–8, 61, 73
Israel, 47

145

Strategic Arms Limitation Talks
   (SALT), 27, 29, 126
Strougal, L. 63, 67–8, 76, 90, 107

Tito, J.B., 19–20
Togliatti, P., 21
trade unions, 107, 112; in
   Czechoslovakia, 89, 98–9
   Poland, 12, 84–6, 108–10
   Romania, 92

Ulbricht, W., 98, 106, 113
United Kingdom, 39, 52, 92, 110
United States, 20, 23, 35–6, 40,
   47–9, 62, 91, 103, 110–11

Vatican, relations with:
   Czechoslovakia, 45
   Poland, 40–1, 115
Verdet, Prime Minister, 50–1
Vietnam, 47
Vietnam war, 23, 39, 115
VONS (Committee for Unjustly
   Prosecuted), 88–9, 94

Walesa, L., 86, 109, 137 n.10
Warsaw Pact, 22–3, 26, 31–3,
   102–4, 111, 121–2, 124
   Czechoslovakian view of, 23,
   43–4
   Polish view of, 103
   reform of structure, 25, 32
   Romanian view of, 22–3, 47, 50
World Bank (IBRD), 47–8, 70–2
Wyszynski, Cardinal, 86, 96, 109,
   115

Yugoslavia, 3, 6, 21, 37, 39, 42,
   47–9, 63

THE LIBRARY
ST. MARY'S COLLEGE OF MARYLAND
ST. MARY'S CITY. MARYLAND 20686